Ibn Battu

MAKERS OF ISLAMIC CIVILIZATION
Series Editor: Farhan A. Nizami

The books in this series, conceived by the Oxford Centre for Islamic Studies and jointly published by Oxford University Press and I.B. Tauris, provide an introduction to outstanding figures in the history of Islamic civilization. Written by leading scholars, these books are designed to be the essential first point of reference for study of the persons, events and ideas that have shaped the Islamic world and the cultural resources on which Muslims continue to draw.

Ibn Battuta

L.P. Harvey

Oxford Centre for Islamic Studies

I.B. TAURIS
LONDON · NEW YORK

Published in 2007 by I.B. Tauris & Co. Ltd. and Oxford University Press India
in association with the Oxford Centre for Islamic Studies

I.B. Tauris & Co. Ltd.
6 Salem Road, London W2 4BU
175 Fifth Avenue, New York NY 10010
www.ibtauris.com

In the United States of America and Canada distributed by
Palgrave Macmillan, a division of St. Martin's Press
175 Fifth Avenue, New York NY 10010

Copyright © 2007 Oxford Centre for Islamic Studies

The right of L.P. Harvey to be identified as Author of this work
has been asserted by the Licensor in accordance with the Copyright,
Designs and Patents Act 1988.

All rights reserved. Except for brief quotations in a review, this book,
or any part thereof, may not be reproduced, stored in or introduced into
a retrieval system, or transmitted, in any form or by any means, electronic,
mechanical, photocopying, recording or otherwise, without the prior
written permission of the publisher.

ISBN 1-84511-394-2
EAN 978-1-84511-394-0

For all territories except South Asia

A full CIP record for this book is available from the British Library
A full CIP record is available from the Library of Congress

Library of Congress Catalog Card Number: available

Typeset in GoudyOlst BT 11.5/13.7
by Eleven Arts, Keshav Puram, Delhi 110 035
Printed in India by De-Unique, New Delhi 110 018

Contents

List of Maps · vi
Preface · vii

PART ONE: THE AUTHOR AND HIS BOOK
1. Ibn Battuta and his *Travels* · 3

PART TWO: PLACES AND PEOPLE
2. To Makka and far beyond · 13
3. India · 25
4. The Maldives · 32
5. To China and back · 41
6. Africans · 67

PART THREE: THEMES
7. Finance and the *Travels* · 79
8. Natural history · 90
9. Women and children · 98
10. The religious framework · 107

Postscript · 116
Further reading · 119
Index · 122

List of Maps*

Map 1:	Ibn Battuta's World	2
Map 2:	Northwest Africa and the Mediterranean in the *Travels*	17
Map 3:	The Indian Subcontinent	29

*Cartography by Alexander Kent, FBCart.S, FRGS

Preface

This little volume does not set out to provide an abridged version of all Ibn Battuta's *Travels*. That would prove to be an uncomfortably hurried scramble, for, as his contemporary (fourteenth-century) editor rightly claimed, 'this shaykh is the traveller of his age'. Ibn Battuta tells us of journeys extending from his native Tangier in the west to Beijing in the east, to Granada and to the Ukraine in Europe, and in Africa to Timbuktu on the Niger, to Aswan on the Nile, and to Kilwa on the coast of modern Tanzania.

It is natural to wish to cast such a great traveller in a heroic mould. The reality is far more interesting. This book does not simply follow the progress through time and through geographical locations, which is what we find in Ibn Battuta's own narrative. After a brief introduction in Part One to the author and his book, and the kind of travel writing to which it belongs, Part Two deals with the principal stages of Ibn Battuta's journeying to China and back, following more or less the order of his narrative. In Part Three key themes are selected for analysis—the means whereby these travels were financed; his wide-ranging observations on natural history; what he tells us of women in the diverse lands through which he travelled. Finally, Chapter 11 is an attempt to arrive at some understanding of the religious framework through which the author moved. The approach enables us to get somewhere near to an understanding of a man who was certainly remarkable, but who was by no means devoid of his share of human failings. My hope is, of course, that some readers will wish to turn next to an edition of the *Travels*, to put the judgements expressed here to the test.

L.P. Harvey

Oxford, May 2007

PART ONE

The Author and his Book

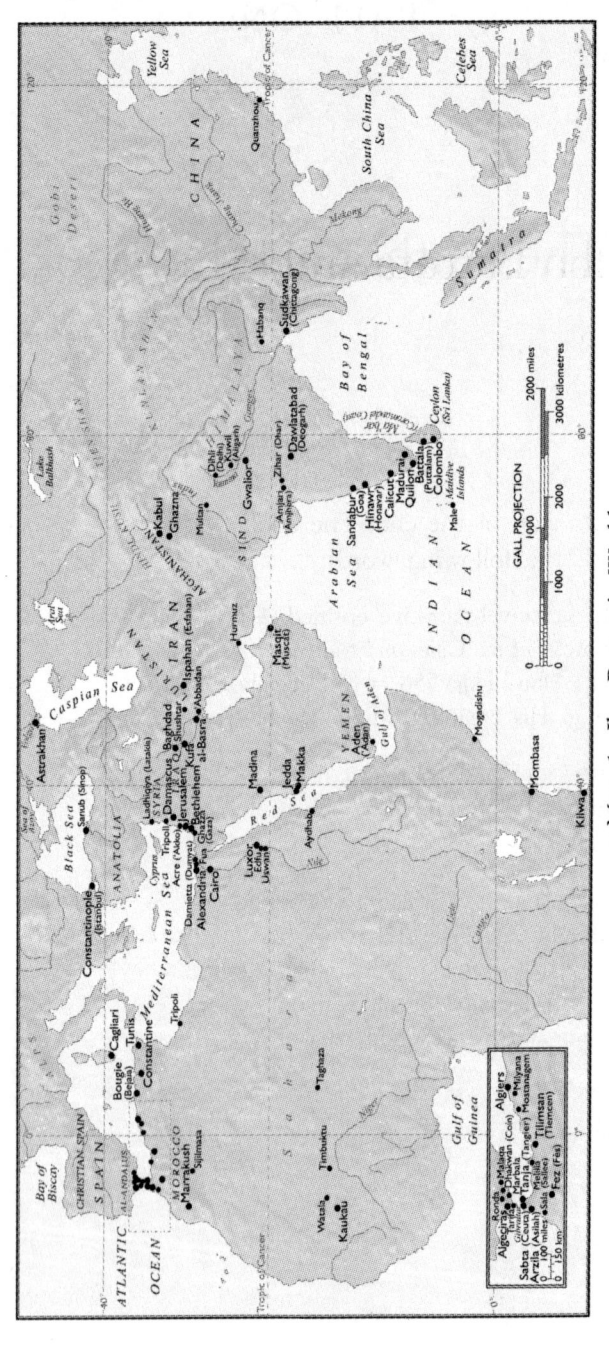

Map 1: Ibn Battuta's World

1

Ibn Battuta and his *Travels*

We need to start at the end. The book of Ibn Battuta's *Travels* closes with the following words:

Here ends the travel-narrative entitled A *Donation to those interested in the Curiosities of the Cities and Marvels of the Ways*. Its dictation was finished on 3 Dhu l-Hijja 756 = 13 December 1355.[1] Praise be to God, and peace to His creatures whom He hath chosen.[2]

Ibn Juzayy (who had been entrusted with the editing of what Ibn Battuta had dictated) then, after some rather verbose remarks of his own, tells us:

Here ends the narrative which I have abridged from the dictation of the Shaykh Abu 'Abdallah Muhammad ibn Battuta (may God ennoble him). It is plain to any man of intelligence that this shaykh is the traveller of his age: and if one were to say 'the traveller of this our Muslim community' one would be guilty of no exaggeration.

Those words bear witness to Ibn Battuta's reputation among his contemporaries as a traveller but they also serve to remind us

---

[1] Ibn Battuta gives us dates according to the Hijri (AH, anno hegirae) calendar, of course. From this point onwards his dates will all be transposed to the Common Era form.

[2] On the translations used, see Postscript (p. 116) and Further Reading (p. 119).

that what we have in the book are not Ibn Battuta's own words, but those of his editor.

A QUESTION OF GENRES

Whereas readers of modern novels appear to be prepared to undertake the disentangling of involved chronologies, readers of modern travel books do not expect to be put to such trouble. From a travel book, readers expect and usually get a coherent narrative arranged in an ordered sequence, and they willingly put their trust in the author's truthfulness. Truthfulness is a characteristic we expect from the genre. (Whether we get it is, of course, another matter.) We modern readers of Ibn Battuta bring to the book our modern ideas of what a travel book ought to be, and when those expectations are not met exactly, we feel baffled.

Literary genres and the boundaries between them do not persist unaltered over the centuries. A late medieval travel writer such as Ibn Battuta (or Marco Polo) was, in his day, catering for a readership with certain expectations—for example that those who went voyaging to distant climes would encounter marvels. The modern reader who enjoys travel writing of the modern kind does not know what to make of a narrative which, while truthful in part, contains accounts of marvels such as could never exist. Another problem for the modern reader is that the identity of the medieval traveller may be just as difficult to pin down as that of the alleged narrator of some 'postmodernist' work of fiction. That is certainly the case with Marco Polo and his *Il Millione* (did he exist at all, or was he just part of somebody else's prose romance?). And so it is with Ibn Battuta. That he really existed is reasonably certain, although one would like to have more independent testimony to his activities than we in fact possess. Yet there are reasons for doubting parts of what he tells us, so that we cannot avoid subjecting to hostile scrutiny his claims to be the author or narrator of 'his' *Travels*. For, as we have just seen, one thing is certain, and that is that Ibn Battuta did not actually *write* a book of travels at all; like some celebrity of the modern age, he told his story to a professional writer, and what we have is what that writer, Ibn Juzayy, made of a professional assignment. It is impossible to state with any certainty when precisely the narrative of the *Travels* began to take shape orally, but with some confidence we may say that the version we have began to come together when, having returned to his native Morocco, after traversing virtually every country then known to Muslims and on occasion adventuring beyond the bounds of that known world, Ibn Battuta recounted at the court of Abu 'Inan in Fez the wonders he had seen. Ibn Juzayy, who wrote it all down for Ibn Battuta, did so under orders from Abu 'Inan. As we have seen, we have a precise date for the completion of that process: 13 December 1355. We will often find ourselves regretting that we do not have equally precise dates for other major events in Ibn Battuta's life.

THE MANUSCRIPT BOOK

Before many months had passed, the manuscript book was copied and complete, and had been given the kind of pretentious long rhyming jingle of a title which was quite usual at this time: *Tuhfat al-nuzzar ghara'ib al-amsar wa-'aja'ib al-asfar*. In 1929 Gibb rendered this as *A Donation to those interested in the Curiosities of the Cities and Marvels of the Ways*, but for the strained Arabic wording many alternative renderings might, of course, be suggested, one being: *For the curious, a rare work concerning wondrous things in great cities, and marvels encountered on journeys*. Such a title hardly accords with modern tastes, and the book—generally known in Arabic simply as Ibn Battuta's *Rihla* ('journey', 'travels'—a term well-established for accounts of long journeys)—will usually be referred to here as the *Travels*.

AN ORAL TEXT TAKEN DOWN BY DICTATION?

To what extent is the book Ibn Battuta's own? When the modern reader learns that Ibn Battuta, when he came to dictate it, did not have available notes or journals relating to his journeyings, suspicions will inevitably be aroused.

A number of points need to be made in this connection. First, and most important, we should acknowledge our modern prejudice against the cultivation of the memory. The educational systems of our modern world, almost without exception, set no store by the training of the memory as such, and indeed most educationalists will decry 'mere rote learning' as something bad in itself, something to be avoided. We moderns therefore have very low expectations of our memories. Nowadays, having been trained *not* to use them (even in elementary arithmetical operations), we are reluctant to accept as true what an earlier age would have taken for granted: that an educated man should be capable of retaining with accuracy considerable amounts of data. Earlier periods have not shared our modern prejudices. Memory has been respected both in itself, and as having an essential part to play in the functioning of all the other mental faculties. There can be no doubt about the importance accorded to memorization among Muslims in the Middle Ages. (And particular respect was accorded to the memorization of the Qur'an, of course.) In that period Islamic educational systems were by no means unique in stressing memory training: memory, as taught, was also important in psychology in the Christian West.

Techniques for the positive training of the memory often exploit the ability which we all possess, to a greater or lesser degree, of recalling *spatial* detail. Some of us are better at it than others, but we can all without exception remember, for example, many details along a familiar path or route, even if we have a bad memory for other things (such as recalling the exact words of a text). One Classical method of memory-training made use of movement through the rooms of a building as a framework to which might be attached details which had to be memorized. Movement through countries in the course of travel is a sequence of data of precisely the same sort. Such material can be coped with relatively easily by a well-trained mind. The length and the complexity of Ibn Battuta's journeys will have presented a considerable challenge to him, but there is no reason to dismiss out of hand as absurd the idea that he might have remembered his *Travels* relatively well without the help of notes. In any case, although Ibn Battuta's sequences of related geographical information (which town, which river came next) are remarkably accurate, some details and even major features are wrong. We are not dealing with a memory feat so faultless as to lack verisimilitude. The book seems to be the product of a sound, even remarkable memory, but not of one that was unusual, certainly not one that was infallible.

Critical appraisal of Ibn Battuta as a travel writer cannot stop at asking to what degree he recorded his experiences accurately and reliably and in sequence. More fundamental is the question of his relationship to Ibn Juzayy, who acted as his amanuensis, and beyond that, to Ibn Juzayy as a professional man of letters, editing, polishing, and adding to what was dictated. The style of the *Travels* is certainly not utterly smooth and uniform. Among the various modes that one can discern are, at one extreme, objective, almost dry reporting, and at the other, high-flown literary purple passages. It is tempting to ascribe what is factual to Ibn Battuta the observer, and what is pretentious to Ibn Juzayy, whose professional pride would make him anxious to improve upon raw material supplied to him. Ibn Battuta might have travelled the world, have rubbed shoulders with the powerful and the mighty, but he had not, up to that time, any reputation as an author. Ibn Juzayy, on the other hand, knew what was expected of him when a work was commissioned by his royal master. We may be certain that some passages were the contribution of Ibn Juzayy, because he says so, and we may judge that some passages retain the traveller's very own words, but between these two extremes there must always remain some doubt about the division of responsibilities. (This problem is discussed further in Chapter 6, concerning Granada.)

What may be demonstrated beyond all shadow of doubt is that long sections of the *Travels* of Ibn Battuta are taken over from the *Rihla* of Ibn Jubayr, a Spanish Arabic traveller who lived much earlier, in the twelfth century. Some descriptions in Ibn Battuta's work, such as that dealing with Damascus, are openly borrowed from this earlier traveller. What are we to make of this circumstance? Is this once again the result of placing the final drafting in the hands of Ibn Juzayy, who knew the established conventions of this genre? Or was it Ibn Battuta himself who was padding out his narrative in this way? Or were the two conspiring together? It is difficult to see how to resolve these doubts.

Even more severe is the criticism levelled against Ibn Battuta to the effect that certain sections of his work are based neither on personal experience nor on earlier authorities but are conjured up from his imagination. If his description of Syria depends on Ibn Jubayr, that is not a grave matter. The debt is acknowledged, and in any case Ibn Battuta had himself travelled extensively in the region, so that although he may have relied too heavily on the work of his predecessor, he is not guilty of misleading the reader with regard to the facts of his travels as such. In the case of his embassy to China, on the other hand, did his voyage take place at all? This question is treated in Chapter 5.

As for Ibn Battuta's constant accounts of the lavish hospitality he received from princes and potentates, it has to be said that at times the boasting about the gifts and payments made to him becomes not only tedious but also incredible. But this was a world very far from our own, and perhaps our standards of what is or is not credible in this respect need to be adjusted. The theme of generosity and hospitality is discussed in Chapter 8.

THE QUESTION OF CREDIBILITY

It would seem we cannot avoid the question of Ibn Battuta's reliability and truthfulness. As Fatma Moussa-Mahmoud pointed out,[3] 'The name Ibn Battuta in Egyptian usage stands for extraordinary feats of travel. It is often used ironically in everyday conversation, 'a new Ibn Battuta' or 'a latter-day Ibn Battuta' meaning 'yet another traveller [who is a] narrator of tall tales!'

[3]Netton, I.R., *Golden Roads, Migration, Pilgrimage and Travel in Mediaeval and Modern Islam* (Richmond, Surrey: Curzon Press, 1993), 168.

Such attitudes are by no means confined to Egyptians. The reputation for truthfulness this traveller enjoys at the popular level is not good. Writing in the same volume as Moussa-Mahmoud, the doyen of Ibn Battuta specialists, Professor Charles Beckingham, 'wholeheartedly agrees'[4] with what she said. Yet it would be outrageously inadequate to write off Ibn Battuta as a trickster and a fraud, even though we find him departing from the truth at some particular points along his way. Ibn Battuta was obviously proud of the reputation he had as a traveller. He lays claim to outstanding status in his field. To use a modern term, he claims to be a celebrity, and after a certain stage in his life, it was as such that he lived, and earned his living. The concept will seem suspiciously anachronistic, and twenty-first century terminology can never fit exactly in speaking of a fourteenth-century man, but the word 'celebrity' does provide us with a useful way to begin to understand what is otherwise an enigma.

The cult of the celebrity is a strange cultural manifestation of our times, but not exclusively of our times. The extreme modern form of the phenomenon is that of the person who is famous for being famous, and nothing more. It is not being suggested that Ibn Battuta was an empty celebrity of that kind. The twenty-first century celebrity is created by the twenty-first century network of information media, above all by television. Nothing like that existed in the fourteenth century, of course, but, already then in the Islamic world, right across the great Eurasian land mass, there did exist a functioning information network of scholars preserving and passing on Islamic learning. Common intellectual tokens passed and were valued and accepted across the continents. The range of information transmitted was restricted to what pertained to the religion of Islam; the speed of transmission, far from being incredibly fast, was limited by the pace of a camel or a horse, but the network functioned as an interlinked information system all the same. It is of the nature of such networks to call into being celebrity figures who safely exemplify the universality of their structures. Ibn Battuta,

[4]Ibid., 86.

'the traveller of this our Muslim community' was famous, not for going where man had never gone before, not for discovering the hitherto unknown, but for knitting together with his scores of journeys, few of which were in themselves in any way out of the ordinary, the whole Islamic world from the Straits of Gibraltar to the Muslim fringes of China, from the ice of the Central Asian steppes to the heat of the African Sudan. In a curious way he became, not for his piety, not for his scholarship, but for his restless journeying the embodiment of the spread of Islam and Islamic civilization world-wide. In the case of many modern celebrities, one is hard put to know whether their reputation rests mainly on their role in public life or their role as entertainers. There is a similar ambiguity about Ibn Battuta. At times he functioned as an Islamic lawyer, but at times his role was to hold his audience and narrate what he had seen. No mere bazaar storyteller he, his were performances put on for the ruling elites. To hold the attention of the powerful, often the all-powerful, cannot have been easy, and was sometimes extremely perilous. The frame-story of The *Thousand and One Nights* provides a tense reminder of the dangers faced by those who practised this craft. On at least one occasion Ibn Battuta had to sit horror-stricken at the dinner table as the potentate he was serving at the time had a poor man's head hacked off. To have a hold over his audience will have been at times as vitally important to him as it was to Shahrazad (Scheherezade). Rather than fables it was tales drawn from life, life as it was lived elsewhere, and incredibly far away, that usually sufficed to enthral his audience; but one of the reasons that Ibn Battuta has been so often seen out of focus, misunderstood, is that his stories have rarely been taken for what some of them are: not so much direct reflections of life's realities, more distractions from those realities.

PART TWO

Places and People

2

To Makka and far beyond

The way in which Ibn Battuta opens his travel narrative invites his reader's sympathy and goodwill. His intention, he tells us, was to visit the holy places, the Ka'ba in Makka, and the tomb of the Prophet (in Madina), but, 'On Thursday 14 June 1325, I set out from my birthplace, Tangier, alone, finding no companion to cheer the way with friendly intercourse, and no party of travellers with whom to associate myself.' He speaks of his sadness at leaving his parents, and theirs at his departure. He was not to see either of them again. His mother actually survived the duration of his travels through the Orient but, although when he at last reached the Middle East on his way back home, many years later, he had news of her, she died before he reached Tangier. (It must be said that the modern reader may well find it strange that he did not hasten back to see her, as he could have done, but one may suppose that neither she nor Ibn Battuta would have felt he would have been justified in missing the opportunity to complete the Makkan pilgrimage once again.)

On his first journey Ibn Battuta would not have remained a lone traveller for long (the pilgrimage brings Muslims together), but it was not until he reaches Miliana in modern Algeria, hundreds of kilometres from his home town, that he speaks explicitly of his travel companions. In Tlemcen, where he had stopped to buy necessities for his journey, he must have had contacts already, for he tells us he was advised there by 'certain of the brethren' about suitable companions for the road: they were 'two ambassadors of the Sultan of Tunis' who were just passing through. The choice of these was hardly an auspicious one, for immediately after he caught up with them near Miliana, both fell ill because of the extreme heat that summer, and one in fact died. Ibn Battuta now proceeded in the company of certain Tunisian merchants. At this early stage in the journey we have to get used to the fact that this travel narrative is no confessional biography. Ibn Battuta tells us in a reasonably systematic way about places he visits, particularly if there are Islamic shrines or other buildings of religious interest there, and above all about the scholars and holy men he meets. He also mentions unfailingly the princes and rulers who welcomed him and helped him on his way, but details about his own material circumstances or about his personal relationships emerge only incidentally. We are often left puzzling over the fascinating fragments that are vouchsafed to us. Thus, for example, at Bijaya (Boujie), he too fell ill, of a fever, and he was advised to stay there to recover. He ignored the advice, and insisted on pressing on, saying he did not want to turn his face from the Hijaz (i.e., Makka) once he had started on the pilgrimage. He was therefore advised to sell his baggage, and to travel light. We can guess that more experienced travellers could see that the young man was encumbered by too much luggage (see Chapter 6). One would much like further information about this first North African stage of his travels. Even more enigmatic is what he tells us, or rather does not tell us, about his relations with the Tunisian merchants mentioned above, and his aspiration at this time to marry the daughter of a well-to-do Tunisian. What were the financial implications? Did he really at this stage have the means to contemplate such a match?

To travel with Ibn Battuta is to travel with a charming, informative and loquacious companion who nevertheless keeps a tight control on what he says, who knows which secrets and confidences he is ready to share, and which he prefers not to disclose. One learns never to expect the whole story from him.

It seems best to listen attentively, and to make what deductions one can from what he is willing to tell us. In part what will seem to the Western reader secretiveness on Ibn Battuta's part may be more his proper respect for the privacy of the affairs of his family, but it is difficult to escape the conclusion that our bafflement also arises from the author's psychological need to keep us at a certain distance. As Ibn Battuta travels further and further away from his home region of North Africa and from the Middle East, we become ever more uncertain that we can understand the purpose of what he was doing. That he took to the roads in the first place to carry out the solemn obligation of pilgrimage to Makka and to seek knowledge is not in doubt, and these were objectives well understood in his society; we, from our cynical modern viewpoint, may think we can identify the pursuit of fortune and of fame as also present as motives (one only has to consider the careful way he sought out the company of the powerful and the well connected), but there comes a point on his travels (it is difficult to pinpoint, but it is well after he has completed his first pilgrimage to Makka) when we may think he has become driven above all by a desire to travel for travel's own sake.

His road towards Makka on his first pilgrimage was not an easy one. He had initially planned to make his way down through Egypt, and cross from one of the Red Sea ports to the coast of the Arabian peninsula. (It is interesting to note that in North Africa and Egypt the ancient pre-Islamic monuments impinge little on his consciousness: his attention is focused on his objective: Makka. Of Luxor he says, for example, 'a pretty little town containing the tomb of the pious ascetic Abu l-Hajjaj.') The pilgrims got as far as the port of Aydhab on the coast not far from the modern Suakin, but, instead of crossing the Red Sea, had to turn back because of the fighting going on in the area, and so they were obliged to retrace their steps and take the alternative land route through Syria. Over this stage in Ibn Battuta's travels it is difficult to disentangle exactly what is going on. The caravan seems to head much too far north up the Syrian coast before going inland to Damascus and then heading for the interior of Arabia. In his 1929 annotations H. A. R. Gibb remarked at this point that Ibn Battuta obviously confused the details of three journeys in Syria. It would seem unsurprising that two decades later he should have made an error of this nature, especially in the case of one of the areas that he visited more than once. He does give us a firm date for his entry into the city of Damascus (9 August 1326), but this is one of the passages where much of the description is not first-hand at all, but is drawn from Ibn Jubayr. Because of his treatment of the storms of controversy surrounding Ibn Taymiyya, whom he claims to have heard preach, we nevertheless get a very lively impression of Damascus as the important centre of religious scholarship that it was (see Chapter 10).

The Arabian section of the journey is dealt with, not summarily but, bearing in mind the importance of the pilgrimage, not at undue length.

We set out at night from this blessed valley [Batn Marr], with hearts full of joy at reaching the goal of our hopes, and in the morning reached, Makka (may God ennoble her!), the City of Surety, abode of Abraham, so dear to God, and home of His chosen one Muhammad, there we immediately entered the holy sanctuary.

All the principal monuments and stages of the *hajj* are dealt with: the Holy Mosque, the Ka'ba containing the Black Stone, and the well, Zamzam. Makka itself and its inhabitants receive due praise: 'the inhabitants of Makka are distinguished by many excellent and noble activities and qualities, by their beneficence to the humble and weak, and by their kindness to strangers', etc. We are told of the generosity shown to religious devotees (who will have vowed themselves to poverty, and so depended on alms), and of how one might rely implicitly on the honesty of the lads who 'for a fixed fee of a few coppers' undertook home deliveries from the markets.

Here in Makka he met fellow countrymen, as in so many places elsewhere in the *Travels*, even in the Far East, encounters with acquaintances from home is a constant theme. Such contacts

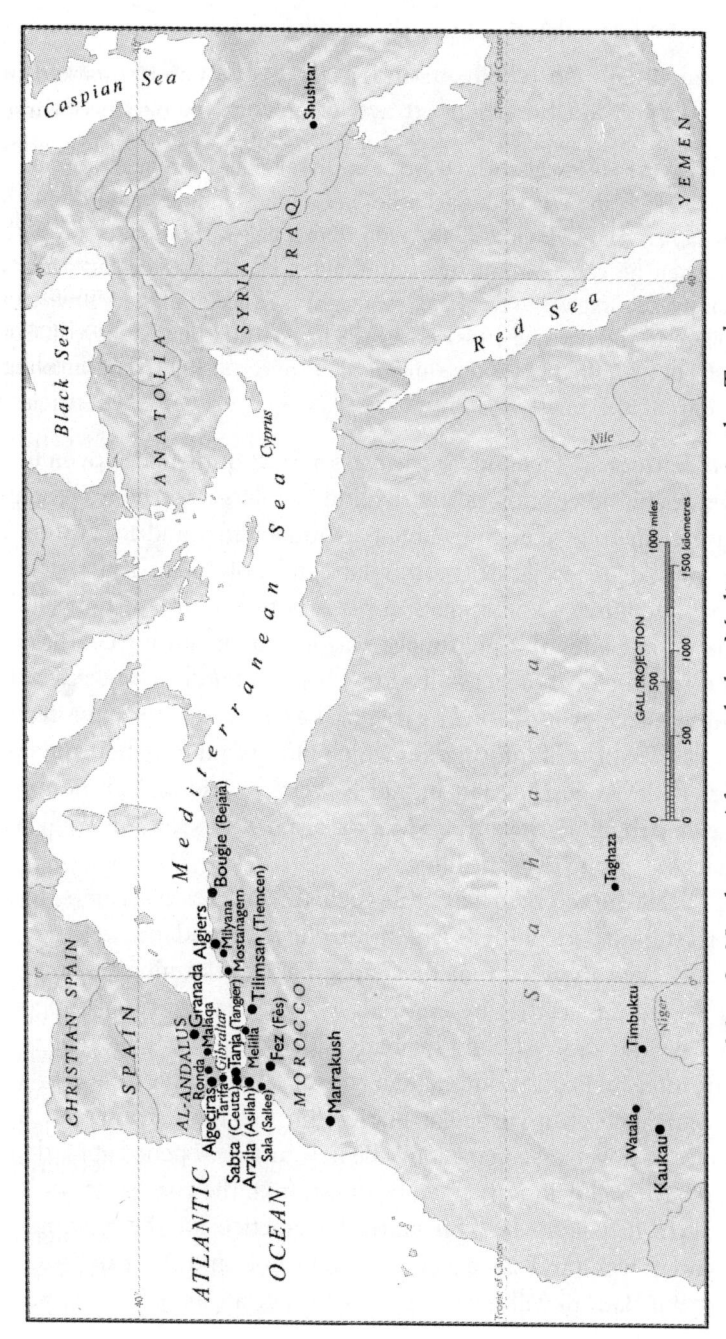

Map 2: Northwest Africa and the Mediterranean in the *Travels*

could usually be relied on to provide assistance and advice: a kind of pan-Maghrebi support network seems to have functioned.

Among the personages who were living in religious retirement at Makka was a pious and ascetic lawyer who had a longstanding friendship with my father, Abu l-Hasan 'Ali al-Anjuri from Tangier. He used to stay with us when he came to our town of Tangier. He had resided in Makka many years, and was to die there. He taught [at Makka] in the Muzaffariya college in the daytime [this was where Ibn Battuta himself stayed], but at night he retired to his dwelling in the convent of Rabi'. This convent is one of the finest in Makka.

Ibn Battuta in fact did not leave for Iraq until mid-November. Besides his description of the city and its rulers while he was there, with numerous anecdotes about its inhabitants and its customs, he provided details of the scholars and holy men. Ibn Battuta was, of course, a young man in his twenties from a distant land; the period after the pilgrimage was an opportunity to establish and reinforce contacts of all sorts. One can hardly over-stress the importance of this secondary role of the *hajj* as a factor reinforcing those networks of information which bind Islam together. Having arrived in August, he left in mid-November, and though he took the land route northwards via Madina again, it was towards Baghdad that the group was heading.

While he was travelling at this period there took place important if mysterious encounters which introduce a fundamental theme of his book: the idea that Ibn Battuta was performing his travels as a vocation so that he enjoyed, in some way, spiritual support in what he did. Already he had told us that at Tlemcen, not long after he first set out, he had consulted the text of the Qur'an for guidance on a particular matter (he was hesitating about his choice of travelling companions: the holy text was opened at random to see what conclusions could be drawn from the passage on which his eyes first lighted). This particular practice for the reading of auguries was (and is) a very common one and we can take it that Ibn Battuta will not have thought it at all superstitious, quite the contrary.

In Egypt near Fua he went to visit a holy man, al-Murshidi. While sleeping on the roof of the hermitage, Ibn Battuta had a dream:

I was on the wing of a great bird which was flying with me towards Makka then to Yemen, then eastwards, and thereafter going south, then flying far eastwards, and finally landing me in a dark and green country, where it left me.

He was puzzled by his own dream, but asked al-Murshidi to interpret it:

You will make the pilgrimage [to Makka], and visit [the tomb of] the Prophet, and you will travel through Yemen, Iraq and the country of the Turks, and India. You will stay there for a long time, and meet my brother Dilshad the Indian, who will rescue you from a danger into which you will fall.

The message that his travels had the benefit of spiritual guidance was reinforced by what happened to him travelling by boat somewhere downstream from Basra. At 'Abbadan he sought out an unnamed hermit whose custom it was to come down to the river bank 'to catch enough fish for his month's provisions, and then disappear.' He found this holy man praying. 'May God grant you your desire in this world and the next,' were the words with which the hermit greeted him. And, as Ibn Battuta says:

I have indeed—praise be to God—attained my desire in this world, *which was to travel through the earth*, and I have attained therein what none other has attained, to my knowledge. The world to come remains, but my hope is strong in the mercy and clemency of God. [emphasis added]

Later that day, the hermit sent Ibn Battuta one of the fish he had caught, with the message: 'This is your hospitality gift.' A modest subvention indeed, but a sort of benediction on the whole enterprise. Clearly what Ibn Battuta would have us believe is that he adopted his life of travel under divine inspiration. There is no indication that he did not himself sincerely believe that; only the cynics among his readers will note how careful he was to choose those roads that would lead him to the courts of princes renowned for their generosity.

Ibn Battuta now entered on a period in the late 1320s and early 1330s of travelling in an apparently random way through the lands of the Middle East. Makka and the pilgrimage provided the firm structure: he returned there year by year after striking out in some new direction, and getting to know some new region of the Islamic heartlands. Sometimes he resided for a considerable period in Makka. In these years, Ibn Battuta was doing three things. He was building up his network of scholarly connections. He was also improving his knowledge of the two great languages of communication in the Islamic world of his day besides Arabic: Persian and Turkish. His Persian must at first have been very weak, his Turkish non-existent. Without these languages he would not have been able to function further eastwards. And finally, he was acquiring experience, on the roads and in princely courts, maturing as a traveller. He made his first *hajj* as a recent graduate fresh from his law studies. By the end of this period he had become a seasoned traveller.

Some idea of the wild changes of direction to be noted in his travel plans at this time may be gleaned from a passage describing what he did after going to Makka in 1332.

After the pilgrimage I went to Jedda, intending to take ship to the Yemen and India, but that plan fell through, and I could get no one to join me. I stayed at Jedda about forty days. There was a ship there going to Qusayr [Koseir] and I went on board to see what state it was in, but I was not satisfied. This was an act of providence, for the ship sailed, and foundered in the open sea, and very few escaped. Afterwards I took ship for Aydhab [on the African coast] but we were driven to a roadstead called Ra's Dawa'ir, from which we made our way with some Bejas through the desert to Aydhab. Thence to Edhfu and down the Nile to Cairo where I stayed for a few days and then set out for Syria, and passed for the second time through Gaza, Hebron, Jerusalem, Ramlah, Acre, Tripoli, and Jabala to Ladhaqiya. At Ladhaqiya we embarked on a large galley belonging to the Genoese.

The galley sailed in south-west Anatolia. That is to say he starts, on the Red Sea coast of Arabia with the intention of going east, he crosses to Africa, and travels the whole length of Egypt northwards, follows the coast through Palestine and Syria, sails by Cyprus to the Anatolian coast, and in the end is travelling westwards!

TO THE GOLDEN HORDE (PERHAPS EVEN FURTHER NORTH), AND THEN TO BYZANTIUM

Among the many peoples of Asia with whom Ibn Battuta became acquainted in the course of his travels during this period was the Golden Horde of the southern Volga region, a considerable power ruled by Muhammad Uzbek (Özbeg) Khan. Our traveller even claims to have gone north from there to Bulghar. This was the capital of medieval Great Bulgaria, situated nowhere near our modern Bulgaria, but near the confluence of the Kama and Volga rivers, and so at about the latitude of Moscow, although some seven hundred kilometres to the east of it. This would be unquestionably the furthest north he reached, and the implications of the latitude for Muslims clearly concerned him: 'We reached it in the month of Ramadan, and when we had broken our fast after the sunset prayer, we had just sufficient time for the night prayers before dawn.' Although the midwinter nights at such a latitude—the rough equivalent of southern Scotland or, in North American terms, the extreme south of the Alaskan panhandle—are short enough, they are not as short as he claims. Is he exaggerating, or is he relying on reports brought back by others from even more northerly locations? Ibn Battuta tells us he would himself have wished to penetrate into what he calls 'the Land of Darkness', forty days march from Bulghar. He knew that travel would have been with sleds drawn by dogs, so if we suppose such a team might have managed at least twenty miles a day, it would indeed have reached the frozen shores of the Arctic Ocean, somewhere north of the Arctic Circle. In such lands, of course, at midwinter there is no sunrise at all. The Land of Darkness would seem a very apposite name.

Ibn Battuta explicitly tells us that he did not manage to make this journey, but he is very well informed about these latitudes. He knows travel is undertaken by rich merchants to procure furs: sable, miniver, ermine. And he has a surprising amount of information about the dog teams, and the very high value of a good dog. 'Its owner never beats or chides it, and when food is made, the dogs are served first, before the men.' There is perhaps a warning for us here. If we did not have his explicit denial that he had made the journey, we might well have assumed that only from personal experience could a Moroccan acquire such a good grasp of the special means of transport used by fur traders in the Siberian Arctic. Ibn Battuta was obviously good at gathering information. So the presence in his book of accurate details about a recondite subject is no proof that the information was acquired first hand. But at the same time we note that Ibn Battuta did in this instance act honestly, and frankly disclaim personal experience. Ought not sceptical modern readers of the *Travels* perhaps be less ready to write off Ibn Battuta's observations as spurious? (On his attitude towards the Russians, see Chapter 6.)

It is certainly very difficult on balance not to dismiss what Ibn Battuta claimed was his next great journey—from the Volga to Constantinople. This is not to say that the case against accepting this part of his narrative is conclusive. Charles Beckingham summed the situation up judiciously, and his words merit quoting. This was one of

> a number of narratives that contain nothing that is physically impossible, which are nevertheless suspect because they cannot be reconciled with what we know from other sources, but which contain details seeming to validate them because it is hard to imagine why they should have been included if the story were not true... '[Ibn Battuta] claims to have accompanied a Byzantine princess, one of the wives of Özbeg Khan of the Golden Horde, on a visit to Constantinople that she had arranged so that she could give birth to the child she was expecting in the palace

of her father, the Emperor Andronicus III. This is by no means impossible, indeed we know that a daughter of the Emperor was married to Özbeg. But when we are told that the Pope visited Constantinople every year, that the Emperor went to receive him when he was four nights journey from the city, walked in front of him when he entered, and came to salute him every morning and evening during his stay, we are bound to wonder whether the whole visit has not been fabricated... Suspicion is enhanced when he describes how he met the deposed Emperor Andronicus II who must have been dead at the time.

One cannot but agree with Professor Beckingham. One can imagine all sorts of possible explanations for the unlikely elements in Ibn Battuta's account. Did Ibn Battuta, who certainly had no Greek, misunderstand a lot of what was going on around him in Constantinople? Inevitably so. Perhaps the man he thought was identified to him as the Emperor was somebody else. Perhaps the 'Pope' in question was a simple Greek Orthodox *papas*. And perhaps the 'former king George' he met when out walking one day, and identified for him by his guide with the words 'this is the king's father' was simply some other holy father.

He took my hand and said to the Greek (who knew the Arabic tongue), 'Say to this Saracen (meaning Muslim) I clasp the hand which has entered Jerusalem, and the foot which has walked within the Dome of the Rock and the great church of the Holy Sepulchre and Bethlehem,' and he laid his hand upon my feet, and passed it over his face. I was astonished at their good opinion of one who, although not of their religion, had entered these places.

We can recognize two themes being conveyed in this episode: they recur in the *Travels* as a whole. In the first place we see how even in the capital of the Christians Ibn Battuta wants us to be aware that he elicited admiration as a noteworthy traveller. But in case this should be misinterpreted as indicating on his part any religious inclination towards Christianity, Ibn Battuta states his second theme: that he steadfastly refused to temporize with religions other than Islam. This he gets across by informing us that he refused to prostrate himself before a Christian altar when told he should do so. The picture he presents of Constantinople is not a hostile one: he is well received, he is interested to see the 'marvellous and rare sights', and he finds the city impressive. Then, when the Byzantine princess he had been escorting makes clear she is going to elect to live as a Christian and stay with her father, he makes his way straight back to Astrakhan.

Astrakhan really marks an important turning point for our traveller. If he had followed the pattern of the previous few years as just described, he would subsequently have turned back towards the south, eventually to make another pilgrimage to Makka. He switches direction, however, and without telling us why, begins to make his way further eastwards, through Persia and Afghanistan to India. As we shall see, it soon becomes apparent that prominent among the motives that impelled him in that direction were ambition and a desire to make his fortune.

3

India

If Luristan was the place where Ibn Battuta found his vocation as a travel narrator (see Chapter 7), and Astrakhan the place where he finally turned his footsteps eastwards, India was where he came to know material success, where he became accustomed to the prosperity that he expected from life from then onwards.

To understand Ibn Battuta's success in the sultanate of Delhi, it is necessary to understand the character of the ruler whom he served there: the king of India, Sultan Muhammad ibn Tughluq. It was the reputation of this ruler for great generosity that drew Ibn Battuta eastwards from Iran through Afghanistan, from Kabul ('formerly a vast town, the site of which is occupied by a village inhabited by a tribe of Persians called Afghans', who, so he tells us, were 'mostly highwaymen'), thence across 'the great desert which extends for fifteen days and can only be crossed at one season of the year' in Sind, and so finally to the banks of the Indus, and the confines of the sultanate of Delhi. Muhammad ibn Tughluq was noted for generosity of a particular sort—an insanely munificent open-handedness, above all directed towards outsiders rather than to natives of his own dominions.

[He] makes a practice of honouring strangers, and distinguishing them by governorships, or high dignities of state. The majority of his courtiers, palace officials, ministers of state, judges, and relatives by marriage are foreigners, and he has issued a decree that foreigners are to be given in his country the title of Aziz [Honourable], so that this has become a proper name for them.

A journey to the court of Delhi was thus (as will be discussed in Chapter 9) by way of being a speculative financial venture for somebody like Ibn Battuta. But it was a venture not without danger. 'The king is of all men the fondest of making gifts, and of shedding blood. His Gate is never without some poor man enriched, or some living man executed,' Ibn Battuta remarks. Clearly this was a despotic tyrant who exercised a power untrammelled by most normal constraints, a curious and fearsome amalgam of piety, cultured intelligence, and brutality. Ibn Battuta presents him as nevertheless willing to subject himself to the jurisdiction of a qadi's court, and recounts the story of a man who hailed the King before the qadi for putting the man's brother to death without cause. The ruler is said to have walked to the court, and to have submitted to the qadi's sentence—that the ruler should pay blood money. (The cynical modern observer may see here a successful exercise in public relations bought at a price the Sultan could easily afford.)

However, in spite of all we have said of his humility, justice, compassion for the needy, and extraordinary generosity, the sultan was far too ready to shed blood. He punished small faults and great, without respect of persons, whether men of learning, piety, or high station. Every day hundreds of people, chained, pinioned, and fettered, are brought to his hall, and those who are for execution are executed, those for torture tortured, and those for beating beaten...

The sultan had a half-brother named Mas'ud Khan...one of the most beautiful men I have ever seen on earth. He suspected him of wishing to revolt, and questioned him on the matter. Mas'ud confessed through fear of torture, for anyone who denies an accusation which the sultan formulates against him is put to the torture, and the people consider death a lighter affliction than torture.

This is the regime to join which Ibn Battuta journeyed from afar. He was rewarded with the office of qadi of the Maliki rite, one of the four orthodox (Sunni) schools of law. With only a modest number of adherents of the Maliki school in India, the office will not have been an onerous one for Ibn Battuta. Nevertheless, he played his part, with his colleagues of the other schools, in legitimizing the hateful regime. Muhammad ibn Tughluq was purchasing religious, moral, and intellectual respectability, and Ibn Battuta was a willing participant in that process—nothing forced him to go to Delhi.

Of all the cases of the exercise of arbitrary power by this ruler, he identifies as the most grave the shifting of the capital, lock, stock, and all its inhabitants, from Delhi to Dawlatabad (Daulatabad, Deogiri) some forty days journey to the south. As compared with the grotesque butchery in which Muhammad ibn Tughluq indulged, this may seem no serious matter, and the sort of policy decision that governments properly take from time to time in response to changing circumstances. Since the Sultan was switching the emphasis of his campaigning towards the south of the Subcontinent, the move was not purely arbitrary in the way that Ibn Battuta would have us believe. (He has Muhammad ibn Tughluq decide on the move in a fit of anger against the inhabitants of Delhi because of anonymous insulting missives he received there.) In the history of the world, how many examples are there of capitals being set up for reasons of state policy in unpopular locations in the teeth of hostile public opinion—not least that of Washington? It was not the policy itself but the way it was implemented that was shocking. The anecdotes on this subject with which Ibn Battuta regales us may or may not have a ring of truth about them, but they undoubtedly convey the dread which the ruler inspired in his subjects (and in his Maliki qadi):

He decided to lay Delhi in ruins...[the inhabitants refused to move to Dawlatabad] and his herald was sent to proclaim that no person should remain in the city [of Delhi] after three nights. The majority complied with the order, but some of them hid in the houses. The sultan ordered a search to be made for any persons remaining in the town, and his slaves found two men in the streets, one a cripple and the other blind. They were brought before him, and he gave orders that the cripple should be flung from a [siege engine] and the blind man dragged from Delhi to Dawlatabad, a distance of forty days' journey. He fell to pieces on the road, and all of him that reached Dawlatabad was his leg. When the sultan did this, every person left the town, abandoning furniture and possessions, and the city remained utterly deserted.

It was to this master that Ibn Battuta had volunteered his services in 1334; he describes the scene as follows:

I approached the sultan, who took my hand and shook it, and continuing to hold it, addressed me most affably in Persian, saying, 'Your arrival is blessed; be at ease, I shall be compassionate to you, and give you such favours that your fellow-countrymen will hear of it and come to join you.' Then he asked me where I came from and I answered him, and every time he said any encouraging word to me I kissed his hand, until I had kissed it seven times... He assigned to us pensions, giving me 12,000 dinars a year, and added two villages to the three he had already commanded for me. One day he sent the *wazir* and governor of Sind to us to say, 'The Master of the World says: "Whoever amongst you is capable of undertaking the function of *wazir* or secretary or commander or judge or professor or *shaykh*, I shall appoint to that office.' Everyone was silent at first, for what they were wanting was to gain riches and return to their countries. After some of the others had spoken, the *wazir* said to me in Arabic: 'What do you say?' I replied 'Wazirships and secretaryships are not my business, but as to *qadis* and *shaykhs*, that is my occupation, and the occupation of my fathers before me.' The Sultan was pleased with what I had said, and I was summoned to the palace to do homage on appointment as *qadi* of the Malikite rite at Delhi.

In a half-hearted way Ibn Battuta seeks to present himself to his reader as really interested in domestic projects and pious public works. His elevated standard of living was, of course, entirely dependent on the revenues he was receiving. But he had already acquired a reputation for extravagance. He was allocated a quite princely budget of resources ('100,000 *maund* of wheat and rice to be expended in this year') but still he asked for more, so the vizier had to give him a warning:

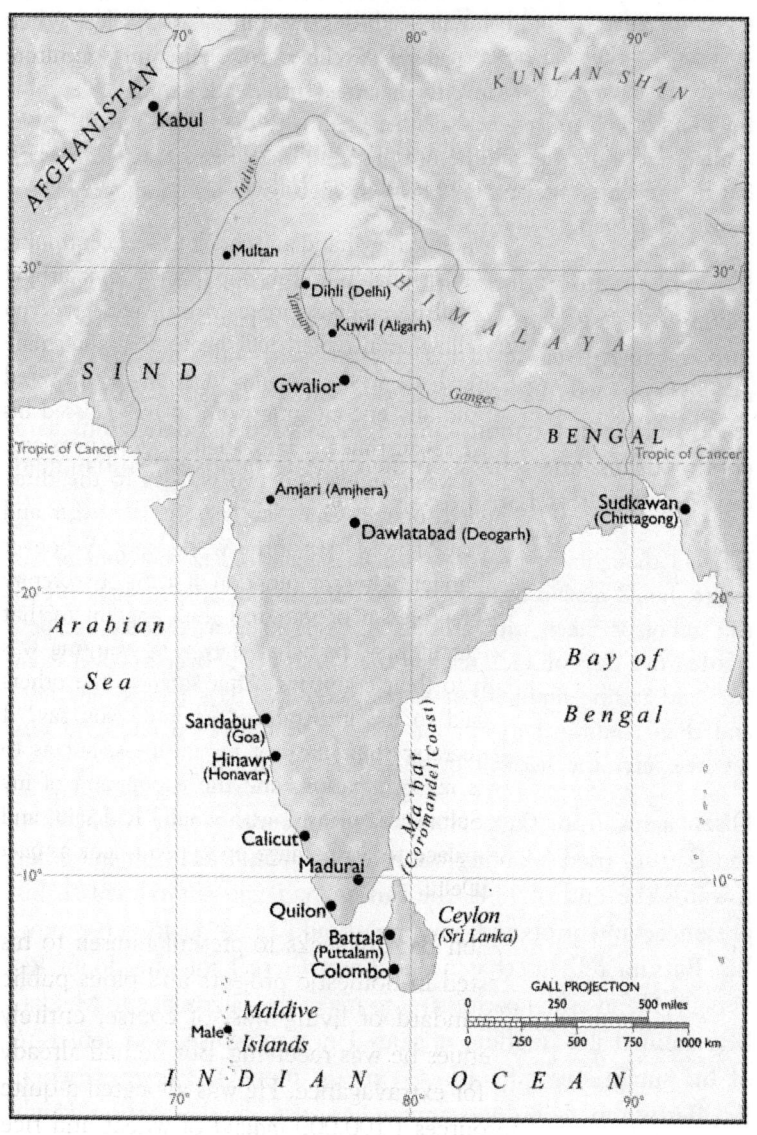

Map 3: The Indian Subcontinent

I asked that my house be repaired. When I had been granted my requests, he said, 'There is another recommendation, and that is that you incur no debts and so avoid being pressed for payment, for you will not find anyone to bring me news of them. Regulate your expenses according to what I have given you, as God has said [in the Qur'an], "Keep not thy hand bound to thy neck, neither open it to the fullest extent." And again, "Eat and drink and be not prodigal." ' I desired to kiss his foot, but he prevented me and held back my head with his hand, so I kissed that and retired.

It is not in the nature of things that anyone should remain in secure enjoyment of the favours of such a ruler. Ibn Battuta fell into disgrace because of his contacts with one Shaykh Shihab al-Din. Here was a sincere religious leader who, in face of danger, stood out against tyranny, who remembered his obligations as a good Muslim, and who soon died at the hands of Muhammad ibn Tughluq. Ibn Battuta only just escaped.

He had thoughts of punishing me, and gave orders that four of his slaves should remain constantly beside me in the audience-hall. When this action is taken with anyone, it rarely happens that he escapes. I fasted five days on end, reading the Koran from cover to cover each day, and tasting nothing but water. After five days I broke my fast, and then continued to fast for another four days on end, and was set free after the *shaykh*'s death, praise be to God.

Disengaging from the service of a homicidal tyrant is not easy. Ibn Battuta tried adopting the role of a mendicant holy man, but towards the end of 1341 the Sultan had him summoned to his presence, and proposed that he should once again serve him. Ibn Battuta tells us that he declined (here I for one doubt his veracity), and asked permission to make the pilgrimage to Makka. Muhammad ibn Tughluq appeared not to refuse, and sent one of his sumptuous gifts (slaves, robes, money). However, when Ibn Battuta made his appearance at court, the destination which was announced to him was not the Holy Places: 'I have sent for you to go as my ambassador to the king of China, for I know your love of travel.'

I discuss elsewhere (Chapter 5, p. 43) the enigma of whether this was a genuine appointment to high office, or merely (as I suspect) a game the tyrant was playing with the mouse he had between his paws. One thing is certain, and that is that Ibn Battuta, after he did eventually get clear of the dominions of Muhammad ibn Tughluq, although he might seek to impress his various hosts by claiming status in the Delhi–Dawlatabad regime, in fact was careful never to return.

4

The Maldives

What took Ibn Battuta to the Maldive Islands? The episode appears almost an aside from the main forward linear thrust of his ambitions. As we will see in the next chapter (Chapter 5), from being a pampered scholar at the court of Muhammad ibn Tughluq in India he suddenly found himself not just without power, influence, or resources, but harried and pursued. That he should be attracted by the idea of taking refuge for a time in a quiet backwater like the Maldives is therefore hardly surprising, although it is infuriating that he really gives us no reason for his specific choice of destination: the Maldive Islands 'of which I had heard' is all he says by way of explanation. And as he tells his story, it would seem that he went there first of all in a mood of depression and despair. We might guess that after the buffeting he received in the dangerous world of Indian politics, the calm of island life at first seemed very attractive. There he was far removed from the great centres of power he had known. Yet his account of the Maldives is full of information, and his witness is particularly valuable because the islands were going though the transition from the period of their initial conversion to that of the consolidation and institutionalization of the new religion. Clearly many other places he visited were relatively less accessible, and the sights he saw in them were more sensational, but what he tells us about the islands is in fact one of the few sources of information about the early Muslim period. And in this easy-going environment (too easy-going for him in many ways, as we shall see) he relaxes his guard at times, and lets us see a little more of his personality.

Because he found the islands and the people (and particularly the womenfolk) so attractive, his observations are sharply focused. Ibn Battuta was no sentimentalist, but when he arrived back in his home region, the Maghreb, the Maldives were, apart from the holy shrines of Arabia, perhaps the only place to which his thoughts nostalgically returned. He remembered the dishes special to the islands, among them a sweet prepared with coconut milk: 'One of the most delicious dishes. I was very fond of it, and used to eat it often.' And he remembered the charms of the women.

The islands, atoll clusters of thousands of low-lying islands stretching for some hundreds of kilometres from west of Ceylon (Sri Lanka) southwards in the Indian Ocean to the equator, had only become Muslim territory in the twelfth century. It was a missionary belonging to the same Maliki school of law as Ibn Battuta, and like him a North African, Abu-l-Barakat al-Barbari, who had brought about their conversion. No doubt a trained Maliki lawyer with some experience of public affairs, as Ibn Battuta by then was, could count on a warm welcome from the rulers of the Maldives, who were seeking to reinforce the Islamic culture of this maritime frontier of the Islamic world. At that stage, in the earlier part of the fourteenth century, the islands still maintained many customs and practices inherited from the not so distant pre-Islamic past.

Elsewhere in the Islamic world, it was not unknown for the inhabitants of some isolated region to try to retain for themselves the services of a qadi by the simple device of detaining (in a literal sense) some travelling scholar. For example, the sixteenth-century North African traveller whom we generally know as Leo Africanus tells us in his travel narrative how he was not allowed to leave a mountain community in the Atlas until he had judged all the backlog of cases that had built up there. Ibn Battuta explicitly alludes to the danger of being pressed into service in this way.

When he arrived on the island of Mahal (Malé), he told the captain of the ship in which he had taken passage to reply 'I do not know him,' if the authorities made enquiries. The precaution was to no avail: news that he had been qadi in Delhi had already reached the island. One wonders whether Ibn Battuta did not really prefer being received as a distinguished guest, and before long we find him reporting the generous hospitality lavished on him by the vizier. This went beyond the provision of luxury food— sheep to roast, for example, which would all have had to be imported, for the islands produced none. He was even provided with a slave-girl (her name was 'Gulistan') who was not a native Maldivian, and so was able to converse with him in Persian 'for the people of those islands have a language of their own which I did not understand'. Ibn Battuta thus did not walk unawares into the trap of being a judge unable to leave his post; he arrived conscious of the danger, and although he took half-hearted measures to avoid being conscripted, in the end he was glad enough to enjoy the respect and attention, the social position, which went with his office. Certainly at one stage he would have preferred to leave, but was obliged to stay on and continue to judge cases, but by then he was of his own free will hopelessly enmeshed in Maldivian politics and business dealings (see Chapter 7).

He did not allow the circumstance that he had been obliged to take up the office to detract from his independence as a qadi. He saw it as his function to introduce the islanders to the Shari'a code in its full rigour. The people who came under his jurisdiction, not to mention the political rulers of the territory, were not always enthusiastic. They were pleased to enjoy the prestige imparted by having a properly qualified qadi, but they were perhaps less pleased at times with his judgements. We shall see that Ibn Battuta had only limited success in tightening up the religious discipline of communities anxious, certainly, to be good Muslims, but not anxious to abandon all the easy-going ways of their ancestors. Ibn Battuta was obviously baffled by a society so different from what he had known elsewhere. He has to acknowledge that these

Maldivians were people exemplary in their honesty and their peaceable conduct, and over and again he remarks on their cleanliness, the frequency with which they wash, the care with which they complete their toilet, their fondness for aromatic oils and perfumes. All this delighted him.

Yet other aspects of life on the Islands he found hard to accept. Perhaps it was the vestiges of matrilineal organization subsisting in social structures that seemed to him fundamentally most alien, but what will have struck him first, in the early days when he had no knowledge of the local language, was the fact that in a community of Muslims who were, as he acknowledged, 'pious and upright', it should be common for women to go about naked from the waist upwards: 'It is thus that they walk abroad in the bazaars and elsewhere.' He is honest enough to tell us that when he obliged some of his own domestic slave girls to wear 'garments like those worn at Delhi, to cover their heads,' it was 'more of a disfigurement than an ornament in their case, since they were not accustomed to it.'

His attempted tightening up of religious discipline did not stop there. One case which came before him created many problems. This concerned a black slave of the vizier, caught in bed with one of the concubines of Jalal al-Din, the Sultan of the Maldives. We are not given enough information about this incident to understand exactly why it evoked such heated emotions, but the essence of the affair was that the vizier wished the judge to exercise clemency, and was 'much agitated and fell into a violent rage' when Ibn Battuta refused to go along with his suggestions. Ibn Battuta insisted on a severe penalty, and had the young man beaten with heavy bamboo rods and paraded round the island with a rope round his neck. His readiness to carry out punishments as laid down by the letter of the law contrasted with the gentler, more lax, regime which he found in force. 'They are unused to fighting and warfare, and their armour is prayer. When once I ordered a thief's hand to be cut off, a number of those in the room fainted.'

COMMERCE, AGRICULTURE, AND OTHER MATTERS

What Ibn Battuta reports about the economic bases of life on the islands does not differ greatly from modern descriptions. 'There is no agriculture at all on any of the islands, except that a cereal resembling millet is grown in the district of Suwayd, and carried thence to Mahal. The inhabitants live on a fish resembling the tunny, which they call *qulb al-mas*.' Ibn Battuta gives details of how it is smoked, dried, and exported. Exactly the same was being reported in the twentieth century, at least until modern transport modified diets by making imported produce available.

What Ibn Battuta clearly appreciated most was the coconut in its diverse forms. It provides, as he put it, 'milk, oil, and honey'. What is more 'all these products of the coco-palm, and the fish they live on, have an amazing and unparalleled effect on sexual intercourse.' And he goes on not only to tell us that, 'The people of these islands perform wonders in this respect,' but to boast of the effect of Maldivian diet on his own life. 'I had there four wives and concubines as well, and I used to visit all of them every day, and pass the night with the wife whose turn it was, and this I continued to do the whole year and a half that I was there.'

The coconut also provided an essential material for the construction of boats and ships: coir rope.

They tan it in pits on the shore, and afterwards beat it out with bars. The women then spin it and it is made into cords for sewing [the planks] of ships together. These cords are exported to India, China, and the Yemen, and are better than hemp. The Indian and Yemenite ships are sewn together with them, for that sea is full of reefs, and if a ship is nailed with iron nails it breaks up on striking the rocks, whereas if it is sewn together with cords, it is given a certain resilience, and does not fall to pieces.

PATTERNS OF MARRIAGE

Some of the marriage customs Ibn Battuta describes must have suited him very well: 'Any of the visitors who wishes to marry may do so, but when time for him to leave, he divorces the woman, because their women never leave the country.' 'It really is a sort of temporary marriage,' he observes. Now as an orthodox Maliki, Ibn Battuta might have been expected to attempt to oppose a custom usually not regarded among Sunnis as acceptable. But as far as the way he arranged his own life was concerned, whether in the Maldives or not, his practice (see Chapter 10) was to divorce and move on. 'It is easy to get married in these islands on account of the smallness of the dowries and the pleasure of their women's society.' 'I have never found in the world any women more agreeable to consort with than they are.' One of the attractions he mentions is that: 'The majority of people do not specify a dowry.' Here again one is surprised at the flexibility of this qadi's approach, for in other circumstances he would surely have felt necessary to point to the essential role played by the dowry in Islamic marriage. The relaxing climate of the tropics perhaps overcame him.

He records what appear to be both matrilineal and patrilineal forms of marriage:

It is their custom that when one of their men marries and goes to his wife's house, cotton cloths are spread on the ground for him...The woman is standing at the door of her apartment awaiting him. Should it be the woman who goes to the man's place of residence, his house is carpeted in the same way...

LEAVING THE ISLANDS

Ibn Battuta does not give us a straightforward and coherent account of why he left the Maldives after his first stay there of more than a year and a half. We must assume that the motives were serious ones. He says absolutely nothing of any hankering for the road again, and it is purely our knowledge of the footloose life he led before and after which tends to make us assume that he never settled anywhere. When he did leave, he was at some pains to give the impression it was for good: he settled his debts, as was required of him by the authorities, and he divorced all but one of his wives. She was the mother-in-law of the son of the vizier 'with whom he was in dispute, and she accompanied him to one of the outlying atolls, where she became indisposed, so he divorced her and sent her back home. (In case it be thought that the qadi was imposing an unduly austere way of life on himself, it is only fair to add that he only continued his journey after sending for 'a slave-girl of whom I was very fond'.)

There are many aspects of this stage in Ibn Battuta's travels which make less than perfect sense. He has told us that Maldivian women never left home: was he using the wife in question as a sort of hostage to secure a safe passage? Far more importantly, did he really set out with the intention of not returning? If he did, it runs counter to what he himself tells us of his political agenda. The incoherence of the narrative at this point may arise from the deviousness which was imposed on him by political circumstances, but my personal suspicion is that he was driven by motives he did not himself understand. If he had been the sort of man to settle down happily for life on a tropical island, he would never have arrived there in the first place. He mentions his disputes with the Maldivian authorities, and principally with the vizier 'Abdallah, over his handling of the case of the black slave found fornicating with one of the Sultan's concubines. It is not unreasonable to assume that this particular case was not the only point at issue between two proud and stubborn men. Ibn Battuta tells us that when by settling all his outstanding debts he had shown beyond a shadow of doubt that he really intended to go, 'Abdallah pressed him to stay. Ibn Battuta would not allow himself to be deflected from his course, and at this point the real motive probably emerges: he was plotting with some of the military commanders against his enemy the vizier 'Abdallah. He was leaving for India to try to incite the ruler of Ma'bar (the Coromandel Coast) to invade the islands.

Like so many enterprises with which Ibn Battuta toyed, this attempt to overthrow the government that he had been serving came to naught, and it was extremely fortunate that the plotting did fail, for the South Indian ruler on whom he was counting, Ghiyath al-Din of Damaghan, proved to be an exceptionally cruel tyrant. Soon after making contact with him, Ibn Battuta must have realized quite how disastrous his error of judgement had been. To authorize those punishments involving the shedding of blood which the Shari'a code calls for did not trouble him (and we have seen that this could bring him into conflict with advocates of clemency), but he found he had no stomach for what was being done quite outside Islamic law by Ghiyath al-Din. He was sitting eating with his new master one day, when an 'infidel' (i.e., Hindu) prisoner and his wife and seven year-old son were brought in, and there during the meal he found himself witnessing not only the summary decapitation of the prisoner, but the cutting of the throats of the wife and child. (Ibn Battuta tried looking away.) On another occasion he guessed from the fact that the ruler's henchmen were drawing their knives that another prisoner was about to be despatched. This time Ibn Battuta excused himself, alleging the need to go to pray the afternoon prayer. 'He [the sultan] understood and laughed. He ordered his [the prisoner's] hands and feet to be cut off, and when I returned I found him wallowing in his blood.'

The fact that the invasion plans were not put into effect owed nothing to any change of heart on the part of Ibn Battuta, who comes out of this whole episode with scant credit. What happened was as follows: Ghiyath al-Din took an overdose of some aphrodisiac pills formulated for him by one of the yogis. They contained iron filings 'to give him strength in copulation', and he fell ill (one presumes with a perforated gut). Ibn Battuta had still not broken with him; on the contrary, he went to meet him with a present. When the ruler 'wanted to give me the price of my present, I refused. I regretted it later, for he died, and I received nothing.' He did in fact receive 300 dinars and a robe of honour from Ghiyath's successor, who was prepared to go ahead with the invasion of the Maldives. The new regime was not a whit less soaked in blood than the previous one. What seems to have persuaded Ibn Battuta to pull out was an outbreak of the plague to which he himself succumbed. This left him depressed: 'I became disgusted with that city, and sought permission to leave it.' The ship on which he sailed away was attacked by Hindu warships and, so he tells us, once more he was robbed: this time he lost everything except his trousers.

At this point he took the extraordinary decision to go back to the Maldives. He must have realized the great danger he was running, and perhaps he would not have taken the risk had he not consulted the Qur'an first, and found to guide him the verse: 'The angels will descend to them saying "Do not be afraid and do not grieve."' The object of this final visit to the islands was to collect the young son he had never seen. Earlier, when he had left, he had liquidated all his family ties in the islands, divorcing his wives, but one had been pregnant, and the child she bore was by now two years old (so he tells us, although it is difficult to reconcile this precise figure with other details, although the discrepancy does not seem of any great moment). The boy had been born while Ibn Battuta was involved in his invasion plots. The mother, not surprisingly, tried to frustrate Ibn Battuta's plan to remove the boy from her custody. The great traveller, if he was to continue on his way eastwards, was really in no position to bring up a young child. Yet Ibn Battuta's erstwhile enemy, the vizier, refused to intervene: 'I shall not prevent him from fetching his son.' So Ibn Battuta went to collect him, but—this is the only aspect of the whole sorry tale which reflects credit on him— at the very last moment he changed his mind. 'My son was brought to me, but it appeared to me that it would be best for him to stay with them, so I returned him to them, and stayed for five days. Thinking it best to hasten my journey, I asked permission to leave.' Of this son we hear no more.

5

To China and back

We must now return to pick up the thread of the narrative of Ibn Battuta's time at the court of Muhammad ibn Tughluq. It will be recalled that at the end of Chapter 3 we left him quite unexpectedly nominated as the sultan's ambassador to China. Ibn Battuta's mission to China is the great puzzle and the great mystery of the *Travels*. As is the case with Marco Polo's overland travels to that country, there are those who deny that Ibn Battuta's sea voyage to China could ever have taken place at all, and there are those who, while ready to admit that he reached the Far East, deny that he managed to travel to all the places he mentions. A prudently conservative view might be that he probably reached South China, but got little further than the ports of the China Sea, and that he pieced the rest together from hearsay and the tales of other travellers.

The reasons why the sceptically minded are reluctant to accept his claim to have got to China by sea are remarkably similar to those for doubting that Marco Polo (whose *Il Milione* antedates our author's *Travels* by perhaps two generations) went there by the overland route. Both these visitors from the west claim while in China to have had dealings with the administration, and to have had important diplomatic missions entrusted to them, and yet in all the written records from this period (which are not lacking), no reference to either of them has ever come to light so far. This has led in both cases to rejection of the China part of the travel narratives as spurious. Both give very incomplete accounts of the China they saw. A recent study of Marco Polo appeared under the title of *Did Marco Polo Go to China?* (Frances Wood: London, Secker & Warburg, 1995); while reaching no firm conclusions, suggests that the European traveller may never have penetrated further east than Venetian trading posts on the Black Sea.

There is no consensus among scholars with regard to Ibn Battuta's claims to have visited the Far East. Attention has tended to focus on the extreme positions: did he go or did he not? Is he telling the truth or he is misleading us? I want to suggest, with great diffidence, because to the best of my knowledge nobody else shares my view, that there is available a possible third position, not a compromise between the other two (that would hardly be logically possible), but one arising from a fresh appraisal of the evidence.

My alternative explanation for the 'embassy' to China occurred to me as I puzzled over an unkind, and indeed dangerous, version of the well-known Indian rope trick which was played on Ibn Battuta by the Sultan of Delhi:

The sultan sent for me once when I was in Delhi, and on entering I found him in a private apartment with some of his intimates, and two of these *jugis* [yogis]. One of them squatted on the ground, then rose in the air above our heads, still sitting. I was so astonished and frightened that I fell to the floor in a faint. A potion was administered to me, and I revived and sat up. Meantime this man remained in his sitting posture. His companion then took a sandal from a bag he had with him, and beat it on the ground like one infuriated. The sandal rose in the air until it came above the neck of the sitting man, and then began hitting him on the neck, while he descended little by little until he sat down alongside us. Then the sultan said, 'If I did not fear for your reason, I would have ordered them to do still stranger things than this you have seen.' I took my leave, but was affected with palpitation and fell ill, until he ordered me to be given a draught which removed it all.[1]

[1]Gibb and Beckingham (1994), 789–90, but here quoted from the abridged version in Gibb (1929), 226.

What this anecdote tells us is that the sultan and his inner circle were prepared to amuse themselves at their pious Maliki qadi's expense.

We have seen that one of the arguments against the authenticity of the embassy to China is that no such diplomatic contacts are mentioned in any of the historical sources. The obvious conclusion to be drawn is that there was no mission and Ibn Battuta is making a boastful claim in order to mislead us. With some hesitation, for I have no fresh source material to adduce, I would suggest that it is also possible that in the matter of the China embassy, rather than himself setting out to mislead us, his readers, he may in the first place have been duped and misled himself, have been the victim of a hoax on a grand scale.

Before looking at the text of this episode in Ibn Battuta's *Travels*, I should mention the story, (it will be familiar to many) which set me thinking on these lines. It is to be found in Cervantes' *Don Quixote*. In the second part of that novel Cervantes develops in various ways the character of Don Quixote's faithful servant Sancho Panza. The peasant comes to aspire to become the governor of an island, no less. The pair, Quixote and Sancho, are at this stage at the court of a duke and duchess who, with their inner circle, amuse themselves quite cruelly at the expense of their odd visitors, and get up elaborate charades designed to discomfit them. The duke and duchess not only have the members of their court target the follies of the madman Quixote, but also of the absurd pretensions to high office of the bumpkin Sancho. He is told he has been granted something he had much desired: the governorship of an island (called Barataria). Courtiers and subservient tenantry cheer his splendid cavalcade as he rides out to take up office, but, to cut the familiar story short, Sancho within a few days learns directly, through the bruises on his own person (inflicted on him, on ducal orders, of course, by strong-arm men), that government and politics is a dangerous business, and so he is only too glad to return to his former humble state.

Now of course *Don Quixote is* nothing but fiction, but it was a fiction reflecting at some removes a social reality. The elaborate joke (*burla*) was a feature of life at some Mediterranean Renaissance courts. The practical joke, often little more than a refined form of bullying, had a special appeal in such authoritarian environments. We have just seen that Ibn Battuta himself, with his story of the levitating yogi, provides evidence that Muhammad ibn Tughluq and his cronies took pleasure in just such amusements too. My hypothesis (and it can never be more than that) is that Ibn Battuta's 'embassy' to China may have started as a very elaborate charade mocking the extravagantly spendthrift qadi's pretensions and bringing home to him his utter powerlessness.

The king of China had sent valuable gifts to the Sultan [of Delhi], including a hundred slaves of both sexes...jewelled garments, etc. with a request that the Sultan would permit him to rebuild the idol-temple which is near the mountains called Qarajil [the Himalayas] at a place known as Samhal to which the Chinese go on pilgrimage. The Muslim army in India had captured it, laid it in ruins and sacked it.

This request (of which there is no hint in any historical source) was turned down by the Sultan, who makes a point from a textbook of Islamic law: permission to build a temple in Muslim territory was granted only to those who paid poll-tax (*jizya*). If the king of China would pay poll-tax that is, acknowledge Delhi's overall suzerainty, 'we shall empower thee to build it.' And at this point in the story, enter Ibn Battuta, who is entrusted with the embassy to China bearing this message and a string of munificent gifts. He does not go alone, of course (nor did Sancho Panza): 'as my fellow ambassadors the Sultan appointed the amir Zahir al-Din of Zanjan [a name which crops up once elsewhere in the *Travels*, but is otherwise unknown to history], one of the eminent men of learning, and the eunuch Kafur, the cup-bearer, into whose keeping the present was entrusted.' Security was assured by a *thousand* horsemen under the amir Muhammad of Herat (a known person, the chief of police) 'to escort us to the port of embarkation', not to mention 'the ambassadors of the king of China, fifteen in number, the chief of whom was called Tursi, along with their servants, about a hundred men. We set out, therefore in a great company with an imposing body of troops.'

Yet within days, so he tells us, Ibn Battuta was in hiding, an isolated fugitive, starving, near naked, and avoiding all human settlements. For a while, to cover himself he did have his old jacket, although it had the sleeves ripped out, but even that was eventually stolen from him. How did such a complete reversal of fortune occur? How did such a well-protected mission disintegrate so totally?

What Ibn Battuta tells us fails to provide any satisfactory explanation. His narrative really makes no sense. The great cavalcade had headed south and somewhat east from Delhi. Its destination (unstated) must have been a port on the south-west coast: that was where the regular trade-route from China reached the Subcontinent. However, there was nothing odd in the choice of a south-easterly direction initially: the route was governed by the need to progress southwards down the valley of the Jumna. Only later did it strike across towards the west coast through Gwalior. But the expedition fell apart well before that, near Aligarh, 'at a pretty town with orchards, most of their trees being mangoes' called Kuwil. What happened was that when they heard that only seven miles away a Hindu force was laying siege to another small town, the cavalcade turned aside to relieve it. This they did very successfully. Whether the Muslims really wiped out 'to the last man' a thousand cavalry and three thousand footsoldiers, while suffering casualties below a hundred seems highly unlikely. As far as the embassy was concerned, the key occurrence was that the eunuch Kafur, custodian of the gifts being taken to the emperor of China, is said to have lost his life. The Muslims sent a despatch back to Delhi asking for further instructions, and meanwhile waited where they were. This proved a most unwise decision, for the Hindus regrouped, and in a small-scale skirmish Ibn Battuta was taken prisoner. The order was given for him to be put to death, but 'a pleasant-looking youth' allowed him to escape.

Is this all elaborate open-air theatre? Ibn Battuta hid up in a thicket (in case the enemy changed their minds), then, moving by moonlight, drinking water from the water tanks, but with virtually no food, he made his way on foot for a week. On the eighth day, when he was extremely weak, a mysterious black-skinned man appeared, a Muslim called 'Joyous Heart'. This man gave Ibn Battuta water and what simple food he had (chickpeas and rice), but Ibn Battuta could travel no further, his limbs were too weak. The stranger hoisted him onto his shoulders and carried him, bidding him to keep repeating the words 'God is sufficient for us, the excellent, the guardian' (Qur'an, 3. 172). When Ibn Battuta came to his senses, he found himself in a safe village, Tajpur, where the governor at least was a Muslim, and so contact with Kuwil could be made. In the governor's care he was fed and given some clean clothing which so it emerged, had been entrusted to the governor by 'a certain Arab from Egypt'. And the clothing turned out to be Ibn Battuta's own, a circumstance which left him, so he tells us, 'extremely astonished' (his readers are too). Then, and only then, Ibn Battuta recalled the prophecy made to him long before by the Sufi Abu 'Abdallah al-Murshidi, to the effect that he, Ibn Battuta, would enter India and there encounter al-Murshidi's brother, Dilshad (a Persian name meaning 'Joyous Heart'), who would deliver him from a misfortune.

I think most modern readers will find this part of the narrative rather tedious. One can only say that such accounts of vague predictions issued by holy men which turn out to be correct must have appealed greatly to Ibn Battuta's audiences, for this is by no means the only such incident in this book. The purpose of the fulfilled prophecy is to suggest supernatural endorsement of Ibn Battuta's eastward progress, to confirm that Ibn Battuta's wanderings were destined, were *meant to be*. At the same time our attention is distracted from the puzzling fate of the embassy.

Clearly the advice given to Ibn Battuta by friends at Kuwil, that he should seek permission to turn back to Delhi, made good sense. (If the hypothesis that this journey started out as an elaborate practical joke executed by the Sultan's entourage is well founded, Ibn Battuta needed to be directed back to Delhi so that the Sultan might enjoy converting him into a laughing-stock.) But if there was an elaborate hoax, it failed, because Ibn Battuta ignored the advice he was receiving, and instead of returning to Delhi pushed ahead with his 'mission'.

He had lost so much. How could he possibly now continue on his travels, which is what his narrative tells us he did? To the modern reader it may seem a kind of psychological fugue, an ever more extreme flight from reality.

From this point onwards Ibn Battuta still continues to put himself forward as the emissary of the Sultan of Delhi, and that name, as he acknowledges, did sometimes open doors for him. But in fact he has no further official contact with his master at all! Even when Ibn Battuta did eventually return from China, it was not to Delhi. In South India on his way back westwards he remained briefly in transit, and then he simply kept on travelling westwards, finishing up home in Morocco.

From Aligarh (Kuwil) onwards and ultimately eastwards, his actions do not make sense. What did he hope to achieve? True, his was an age in which diplomacy had not yet come to be as tightly controlled by the home governments as it is today. The ambassador in Ibn Battuta's time might frequently be on his own, quite out of contact, and obliged unaccompanied to pick a way through real dangers; but there can never have been anything quite like the mission which Ibn Battuta claims to have led.

Whether this perhaps far-fetched hypothesis of the elaborate heavy-handed joke is correct or not, from Aligarh onwards Ibn Battuta's narrative changes character.

If he really did not go to China, this would be a unique case of an author seeking to establish a false claim to have visited a place by saying he stayed indoors and did not go out to look at anything! The passage rings true.

Of course we cannot entirely exclude the alternative hypothesis: that Ibn Battuta never went to the Far East at all. Did he invent the whole journey, or perhaps simply fill out from other sources of information what snippets of information he had collected at first hand? The vividness of some descriptions may make it seem likely that they record what was seen by an eyewitness, but we can never exclude the possibility that what we have is the product of a skilled narrator who knows how to make good use of second-hand data. (Let us recall (Chapter 2) the vividness of his description of the handling of teams of sled dogs in the frozen wastes of Russia, north of Bulghar, an area he tells us he had never visited.) Unless some positive evidence of his presence in China at the right time comes to light—and that now seems unlikely—we have to accept that we shall never know for certain.

Among passages that dispose the reader to accept the account as arising from genuine personal experience is the following:

The land of China, in spite of all that is agreeable in it, did not attract me. On the contrary, I was sorely grieved that heathendom had so strong a hold over it. Whenever I went out of my house, I used to see any manner of revolting things, and that distressed me so much that I used to keep indoors and go out only in case of necessity.

And yet we can well imagine that an orthodox Muslim concerned with the *halal* rules, when confronted with the bewildering variety of unidentifiable meat and other products on display in a food market, might have found his stomach heaving, especially when he saw dogs on sale for human consumption, not to mention ubiquitous pork, of course. (Nor would food have been for the Muslim visitor from outside China the only troubling sight; there would have been all the idols, with their smoking joss-sticks.)

If we look at his account, we see that it was not so much authentic Taoist/Confucian/Buddhist China that he visited as the China of the Muslim minority communities. These may have been, as they still are, only a small proportion of China's teeming millions, but in some places there were very large communities of long standing, capable of providing an alternative network thanks to which the visitor could indeed travel without the need to have too many direct dealings with non-Muslim Chinese. Moreover, the use of Turkic languages by some of these Muslims, their knowledge of Persian, and sometimes even of Arabic would have attenuated the enormous language problem, while at the same time restricting the traveller's freedom of movement even further. Given these circumstances, it is hardly surprising if at times Ibn Battuta took the ways and customs of his Muslim hosts to be the normative customs of China as a whole (as, for example, his description of funeral practices).

Among the many passages which appear based on personal observation is his praise of Chinese skill at portraiture. Interestingly, this was, according to him, made use of in the policing of outsiders in a system of close surveillance which sounds frighteningly modern: 'It is their custom to paint everyone who comes among them. They go so far in this that if a foreigner does something that obliges him to flee from them, they circulate his portrait throughout the country, and a search is made for him.' This all presupposes a highly efficient bureaucracy, and Ibn Battuta has a great deal to say about that: the detailed registration of imported goods, the tracing of travellers' whereabouts night by night, the close accounting for the funds brought with him by the traveller, and so on. In consequence, 'China is the best and safest country for the traveller. A man travels for nine months alone with great wealth, and has nothing to fear.'

We get from Ibn Battuta a clear impression of what it was to travel slowly through this country on its great canals and riverways. In detail the picture may be wrong, with canals being taken for rivers and vice versa, and waterways alleged to exist where there were none. That does not to me seem a reason for rejecting the whole account as spurious. It must be borne in mind that Ibn Battuta did not have the benefit of maps or even notebooks when he came to dictate his travel narrative. It is hardly surprising if it is not now possible to reconstitute a complete itinerary. The general view of a land profoundly different from North Africa and the Middle East is persuasive; the mistakes may be blatant but they are explicable.

Ibn Battuta, like other travellers of the medieval period, was fascinated by the technical marvel of Chinese porcelain. This constituted a valuable part of the Chinese export trade. Baffled experts in the Arab lands and in Europe failed for a long time to penetrate the trade secret of bone china. One can be absolutely certain that if a foreign traveller asked about china pottery he would not get the truth from the Chinese suppliers. What Ibn Battuta tells us is a muddled conflation of the mysteries of porcelain and of anthracite. 'All the people of China and Cathay use for charcoal an earth which has the consistency and colour of clay... They set it alight and it burns like charcoal, but it gives off a more intense heat.' The ashes, he assures us, can then be made into briquettes which will burn again, and so on and on until finally from the remaining exhausted white ash 'they make vessels of Chinese pottery, adding another stone to it as we have related.'

Perhaps Ibn Battuta's account of the use of paper money seems as difficult to believe as his account of renewable fuel:

The people of China do not do business for dinars and dirhams. In their country all the gold and silver they acquire they melt down into ingots, as we have said. They buy and sell with pieces of paper the size of the palm of the hand which are stamped with the Sultan's stamp. ... If these pieces of paper become tattered from handling they take them to a house which is like our mint, and receive new ones instead.

An unlikely traveller's tale, many of his readers will have thought.

The tempo of Ibn Battuta's exit from China is an accelerated one. The reader is given little time to reflect on what is happening. The narrative (is it the decision of Ibn Battuta himself, or that of Ibn Juzayy?) brings the traveller back to the west with the minimum of explanations. In North China, Ibn Battuta was advised to leave as quickly as possible because the country began to sink into civil wars in which the emperor died. Ibn Battuta certainly gives a garbled account of the personalities involved in these complex internecine struggles, but his impressive description of the barbaric pagan funeral rites of the Mongols for their ruler appears to correspond to ethnographic realities. Ibn Battuta did not create the scene from his imagination; if he did not see the ceremonies himself, he had contact with somebody who did.

The city [Khan-Baliq, i.e. Beijing] was decorated, drums were beaten, trumpets and bugles were played, and amusements and entertainments were organized for the space of a month. Then the bodies of the dead Qan and about a hundred of his cousins, relatives, and intimates were brought. They dug a great *na'us*, that is, underground chamber, spread with the finest carpets. The Qan and his weapons were placed in it, with the gold and silver vessels from his palace. Four slave-girls and six of his favourite mamluks with jars of drink were placed with them. Then the door of the chamber was built up, and earth was piled over it all until it reached the size of a large mound. After that they brought four horses and drove them about the Qan's grave until they collapsed. They then set up a wooden structure over the grave, and fixed the horses to it after first driving a wooden stake through each horse from tail to mouth. The aforesaid relatives of the Qan were placed in subterranean chambers along with their weapons and household vessels. Over the graves of the great men among them, of whom there were ten, they impaled three horses each, and over the tombs of the rest, one horse each. This day was observed as a solemn holiday. No one stayed away, neither man nor woman, Muslim nor infidel. They all wore mourning, which means white capes for the infidels, white robes for the Muslims... I do not recall any other nation except this follows these practices in our time.

Scarcely have we had time to take in this stark Central Asian barbarity when we are told of Ibn Battuta's arrival back at al-Zaytun (Quanzhou), the South China seaport used by the junks that sailed to India. There Ibn Battuta was fortunate enough to find a junk from Sumatra with a Muslim crew; he was even recognized by the shipping agent. And so via Sumatra he made his way to Kawlam (Quilon in South India), and on to the Persian Gulf and Hormuz. Thence by land he began to traverse roads he had travelled on the outward journey, and through Isfahan and Basra (where among other tombs he visited that of Malik ibn Anas), to the shrine of 'Ali ibn Abi Talib at Najaf, and Kufa, finally to Baghdad. There he caught up with some of the news of his native region, the Islamic West. The Christians at Tarifa in 1340 had defeated the Marinids (who had crossed over to the Iberian peninsula from their native Morocco) and taken Algeciras (1344). He discovered more personal news upon making enquiries when he reached Damascus, a city he had last seen twenty lunar years before, in 1326. 'I had left there a pregnant wife,' he informs us now—characteristically, this is the first we have heard of it! She had given birth to a son, that much he knew already (although he had not felt it necessary to apprise his readers of the fact earlier). Once in Damascus on this occasion, 'I had no other concern than to ask after my son,' he relates, in a tone which seems to call for admiration for his paternal solicitude. He learnt that the child had died twelve years before. (Of the boy's mother we are told nothing.) Ibn Battuta's father had also died many years before, but, he learned, his mother was still alive in the Maghreb. (He was not to see her alive.)

Ibn Battuta visited the shrines and holy places of Syria and Palestine once more, and then turned for the pilgrimage to Makka. This was 1348, the Black Death was raging in most places he visited, and many were the scholars and legists whom he had got to know on his earlier travels who had died in this dreadful plague. When he got to Cairo, he reports, the number dying there daily was 21,000! 'I found that all the *shaykhs* I had known were dead.' The plague did not deter Ibn Battuta from making the pilgrimage to Makka, which he did via Jedda (1348), leaving by land via Jerusalem. By 1349 he was sailing westwards at last. The small boat which landed him at Jerba in Tunisia was to be taken by pirates. From Tunisia it was in a Catalan ship that he sailed. He was understandably jumpy when it put in to Sardinia, but the voyage continued safely to Tenes and Mostaganem. He was now in his home country, but not yet safe! In the general area of Melilla, he tells us, he and his companions had to fight off an attack by fifty men on foot and two horsemen. He does not identify his assailants, but we may guess that they were Berber tribesmen. On 6 November 1349 he at last entered Fez.

In this section of the *Travels* we find, quite understandably, effusive praise of the Merinid ruler, Abu 'Inan, far too fulsome for modern tastes: 'His majesty caused me to forget the majesty of the Sultan of Iraq, his beauty to forget that of the king of India,' and so on. It is the turn of local pride and Maghrebi patriotism:

I laid down my travelling staff in his [Abu 'Inan's] noble country after verifying with superabundant impartiality that it is the best of countries.

...The poet spoke well who said:

The West is the best of lands as I can prove.
The full moon is near to it and the sun runs thither.

The active participation of the *littérateur* Ibn Juzayy is obvious enough in these pages, and indeed a number of the passages are directly attributed to him. The effect is tedious rather than touching. The narrative, in the panegyric mode, fails to tell us what we would like to know: Ibn Battuta's personal reactions after coming back home after so long an absence.

Tangier, his native town, he saw, and Ceuta, where he had to remain 'for some months' because he fell ill there. This illness at least provides an explanation of his motive in now going on to Spain. It would seem that in gratitude to God for curing him, he wanted to take part in the holy war against the advancing Christians. He disembarked just after the death of Alfonso XI of Castile, which took place on 20 March 1350.

Ibn Battuta's account of his travels in Andalusia is short, even in proportion to what must have been a relatively short visit, but it merits as close attention as any part of the *Travels* because it has characteristics which mark it off from the rest of the work. This is Ibn Battuta's only venture into western Europe, but that is not the reason: the isolated kingdom of Granada, as he described it, would not have seemed outlandish to his readers elsewhere in the Islamic world. Indeed it was, in the first half of the fourteenth century, culturally and economically still closely tied in with North Africa and the East. Much of what Ibn Battuta has to report serves to confirm that this was a land not very different from Islamic North Africa across the water, or indeed Arab lands further afield. As for the Christian states of the rest of the Iberian peninsula, these he does not even attempt to visit.

What makes this passage in the *Travels* one of key importance in the book is not so much the intrinsic interest of the descriptions of this last bastion of Islamic Spain (al-Andalus)—although this is considerable—but the help it gives us in tackling the larger question of whether or not we may accept as true what Ibn Battuta tells us in the book as a whole. This is because it brings us some information in a perspective different from that of the rest of the book. Information on other parts of the world is mediated to us through Ibn Battuta's narrative as edited by Ibn Juzayy, a Granadan scholar earning his living at the Merinid court in Fez. The reader would like to know where the contribution of the author ends, and that of the editor begins, but it is difficult for him to judge. In the section on Granada itself, however, things are different. Ibn Juzayy ceases in certain passages to be a mere editor, ghost writer, or whatever his role may have been, and briefly appears as himself. It is no more than a fleeting glimpse that we catch of him in this other perspective, but it is one which is of great assistance to us in forming a judgement both on the general reliability of what Ibn Battuta is telling us elsewhere, and on the role of Ibn Juzayy himself. What sort of a writer was this editor, silent most of the time? How would he handle material if left to his own devices? Perhaps with care we may even come to detect his tone of voice, and to recognize it when it makes itself heard elsewhere in the narrative. At least we can form some idea of what were his literary preferences and stylistic habits.

Ibn Juzayy 'wanders into shot', as it were, when, as a member of the circle of admiring listeners clustered round Ibn Battuta, the by then world-famous traveller, tells an assembly of distinguished Granadans, mainly jurists, about his travels. Ibn Battuta had been unable to secure an audience with the Sultan of Granada (of that more below), and he was invited to attend an all-night literary party (perhaps organized for him as a consolation for not seeing the Sultan?), a memorable gathering in the garden of 'the jurist Abu l-Qasim Muhammad, son of the jurist and eminent secretary Abu 'Abdallah b. 'Asim.

'We stayed there for two days and a night.' This was clearly the sort of grand reception and protracted entertainment in which people in many parts of the Arab world have always taken delight, and Granada had, and still has, so many splendid settings for such occasions.

Ibn Juzayy remarks:

I was with them in that garden. Shaykh Abu 'Abdallah [i.e. Ibn Battuta] *delighted us with the story of his travels.* I took down from him the names of the famous people he had met, and we profited greatly from him. A group of the notable people of Granada were with us, among them the gifted poet, the remarkable Abu Ja'far Ahmad b. Ridwan b. 'Abd al-'Azim al-Judhami. The story of this young man is astonishing. He grew up in the countryside, did not study or frequent the learned, yet he came to write excellent poetry of a quality rare among masters of eloquence and eminent men of letters, for example:

You who have made my heart your home, its door is the eve that glances at it, My insomnia opened the door after you left. Send your spectre who will lock it.

We can see here that, although Ibn Juzayy was very proud and pleased to have been present on such a memorable occasion as the night Ibn Battuta met the cream of Granadan literary and intellectual society (the principal guests are named and identified for us), he was not so overwhelmed as to fail to mention that as well as the overseas visitor, the local star poet al-Judhami was there, and that he recited his own verse. This inward-turning tendency of Granadan intellectual life (together with the pleasure taken by the men of letters of that city in meeting in literary academies and assemblies) is a characteristic which is still alive today. Granadans have rarely been willing to concede that the literary talent of outsiders could really rival the home-grown product. Nor could anything match a well-turned poem replete with ornate rhetorical flourishes and elegant conceits.

Elsewhere in this short section on Granada, Ibn Juzayy found cause to quote much more poetry. Mention of Gibraltar, for example, brings to his mind a poem written nearly two centuries earlier by a Valencian poet, Abu 'Abdallah b. Ghalib, on the subject of the deeds of the first of the Almohad caliphs, 'Abd al-Mu'min ibn 'Ali, the ruler who fortified the Rock. This poet, so Ibn Juzayy assures us, described Gibraltar 'with unprecedented elegance'. There are six such mannered poetic passages quoted, one of them ten lines long. In Ibn Juzayy's hands, the prose narrative of Ibn Battuta's visit is in process of being transmogrified into an anthology of verse about places in the kingdom of Granada. This section thus comes to resemble the many other works of literature in which verse ornaments the prose content, and indeed often comes to assume greater importance than the narrative which it accompanies. (Perhaps the best known example of such a compilation is the North African al-Maqqari's *Nafh al-Tib*—an anthology and historical memoir loosely structured round the theme of al-Andalus—but scores of examples might be cited.) If the whole of Ibn Battuta's book of travels had been subjected to a process of intensive poetic exemplification and ornamentation similar to that in the chapter on Granada, I think that the twenty-first century reader of the text would find it much more difficult to approach. (There is the other, allied consideration, that the very highly mannered poetry of this period is difficult to translate at all, almost impossible to translate so as to produce readable English verse. In consequence, if the travel narrative had everywhere been as stuffed with literary plums as is the section on Granada as edited for us by Ibn Juzayy, the resulting dish would in translation have become quite indigestible.) We do not find verse quotations used in this intensive way in the book as a whole, only in this Granadan chapter. I, and perhaps other modern readers, may feel that Ibn Battuta the prose narrator is not well served here by Ibn Juzayy the man of verse and the cultivator of *belles lettres*, but tastes change, and the treatment accorded by Ibn Juzayy to the material provided to him may have been what was necessary if it was to be accepted as a serious work of literature, and not just a mere oral entertainment. (Another passage where Ibn Juzayy's literary tastes similarly threaten to unbalance Ibn Battuta's narrative comes when, in describing Damascus, he makes use of an extensive extract in rhetorical rhyming prose (*saj'*) taken over from the description of that city in the *Travels* of Ibn Jubayr, but that is a different matter. With

Damascus, Ibn Juzayy (if it is he) simply adopts and adapts the text of his predecessor.)

The striking stylistic difference between this section describing Ibn Battuta's visit to Spain and much of the rest of the book therefore serves to reassure us about the general authenticity of the work as a whole. In this chapter, the editor, knowing the subject-matter better than his author, feels entitled to take over command, and to ornament as he (and not Ibn Battuta) sees fit. How could one write about such a beautiful city as his without quoting from its rich poetic tradition? In consequence, in those places where such poetic gloss finish has not been applied, we may feel more confident that we may have the *Travels* as the traveller himself intended. We have no absolute assurance, of course, for any argument based on *absence* of evidence, absence in this case of ornamental verse, cannot be a strong one. But nobody can read this particular chapter and fail to note that the editor here set about his task in quite a different way.

It would be wrong to imply that Ibn Battuta was not himself interested in poetry. There are a number of references by him to poetry recited or performed in various locations, but these are not decorative verse quotations, they are something quite different, they are, as it were, the field observations of an anthropologist *avant la lettre*. What he is interested in is details such as the peculiar voice register used in some cultures by poets and bards, or the content of African praise poetry, or the strange ceremonial circumstances of poetical recitals and performances. He does not actually cite verse, and almost the only lines we are given outside this chapter are the Persian words (identified for us by Professor Beckingham as being from Sa'adi) which he was forced by his host 'the great amir Qurtay' to learn by heart during a long and presumably convivial party on a pleasure-boat on a 'canal' in China. (That the canal, so modern editors assure us, does not exist, is not relevant to our present purposes.) I think it is not unfair to say that for Ibn Battuta metrical compositions in verse were an interesting cultural manifestation, but that he lacked that consuming passion for Arabic poetry which we find in so many writers, even writers on subjects far removed from poetry itself. Ibn Juzayy, on the other hand, had that passion, and like any Andalusi, his preference was for the poets of his native land.

Let us now tackle the awkward fact about Ibn Battuta, that not only did he go to Spain and see nothing of Christian territory, he went to Granada and did not see either the Alhambra or the Generalife. What sort of a record is this for a champion traveller?

It has to be said in Ibn Battuta's defence that in the fourteenth century, of course, the Alhambra was not a public monument kept open as a museum by the Patrimonio de la Alhambra, but was the securely guarded palace of an absolute monarch. Yusuf I on the whole enjoyed the respect of his people. His reign from 1333 to 1354 was a comparatively long one, but let us not forget that he had good reason to keep out strangers. His reign came to an abrupt end when he was assassinated in the Great Mosque in Granada just after completing his prayers. The historian Ibn al-Khatib[2] writes his assassin off as merely 'crazed' *(mamrur)*, but, whatever the nature of this particular assailant, Yusuf would not have thrown his palace open to a mere 'traveller', even such an illustrious one as Ibn Battuta. If Ibn Battuta had arrived as a personage of political consequence, if he had borne an embassy, he would have found himself summoned to an audience chamber, and might have managed to glimpse at least corners of the interior of the Red Palace.

Of Yusuf I he tells us: 'I did not meet him because of an illness he had, but his nobly born, pious and excellent mother sent me some gold dinars, of which I made good use.' That the sultan should have made his excuses is not strange. A head of state is hardly obliged to spare time for all visitors to his capital. It is even possible that the illness was the plain truth. Gibb, when in 1929 he published his selections from the *Travels*, objected that 'The nature of his malady does not appear to be mentioned

[2] Ibn al-Khatib, Lisan al-Din, *Kitab a'mal al-a'lam* (Rabat, 1934), 352.

by other writers.' One can hardly expect every indisposition, even of an autocrat, to be recorded for posterity.

What we cannot help noticing is that, if we are to trust the text of the *Travels*, the ruler of virtually every country visited by the traveller *did* receive him, unless there was a war raging at the time (as was the case in China when he arrived to see the Qan). Usually the welcome is reinforced by a conspicuous display of generous hospitality. Is it not a little suspicious that on the one occasion when his editor was present as a witness, and so able to tell us exactly what did happen, the hoped-for audience was not forthcoming? What the Sultan of Delhi and the Emperor of Constantinople (and in China the 'principal emir' Qurtay), had managed to find time for in the midst of all their other preoccupations, could not be fitted into the schedule of the Sultan of Granada! Those of a disbelieving turn of mind may find themselves going on to wonder whether Granada was indeed the only country where Ibn Battuta was treated in this way. Is it possible that the stories of royal welcomes lavished on him, of emperors coming out to escort him, and so on, were a necessary part of the advertising material of someone who was, whatever else he may have been, an itinerant entertainer and a public performer of considerable talent? One recalls those circus entertainers who have always appeared 'before the crowned heads of Europe'.

There might have been another reason for Yusuf I keeping Ibn Battuta at a distance: suspicion. As we read the text of the *Travels*, we form an idea of the fighting in Spain between Muslims and Christians as a simple two-dimensional conflict, with the forces from Ibn Battuta's native Morocco and the Granadans in indissoluble alliance on one side against their Christian enemies. In fact there was taking place over this period a most complex and multi-dimensional series of shifts in alliances, with the powers manoeuvring for control of the Straits of Gibraltar and the southern corner of the Iberian peninsula. North African support for their threatened coreligionists to the north of the Straits was until the end an essential element in the defensive struggle on the frontiers. Granadan statesmen, Yusuf I among them, were always conscious that whenever in the past North Africa had been called in to stem the Christian tide (as in the time of the Almoravids and then of the Almohads), al-Andalus had ended up annexed by its North African saviours (usually with the former rulers of al-Andalus in prison in North Africa). To muster sufficient help from overseas without losing one's independence was an essential skill required of any ruler of Granada: it was a tightrope very difficult to tread. Yusuf had that skill, and in a reign of just over two decades 'presided over what was undoubtedly the Golden Age of Granadan cultural achievements'.[3] Ibn Battuta, we know, had arrived back in the West with his reputation as a traveller established. We may wonder whether he did not also bring with him a reputation of another kind as well. In the Maldives we have seen him in action as a dangerous political trouble-maker, stirring up a rebellion. Was perhaps that reputation brought to Yusuf's attention? Is it surprising that the ruler of a state in the perpetually precarious situation in which Granada was placed should prefer to keep him at a safe distance?

In many of the frontier areas which he visited elsewhere in the world, in Asia and Africa, rulers were delighted to welcome this well-trained Arabic-speaking scholar and jurist, and, if they could, to attract him to take up residence for a time as an intellectual ornament at their court, a visible sign that their outpost of Islam was linked fully to the world-wide Islamic scholarly community; they were willing to pay him handsomely for his services. Granada under Yusuf I was on the frontier, and in a precarious situation, but its inhabitants did not have any doubts about the superiority of their culture. Until the very end (and beyond the end), Granada saw itself as the inheritor of the glories of al-Andalus. In their exile, this intellectual superiority complex of Granadans often created difficulties for them in their dealings with North Africans (something of this tension still subsists even nowadays, for the

---

[3] L.P. Harvey, *Islamic Spain: 1250–1500* (Chicago: University of Chicago Press, 1990), 190.

'Andalus' are still in some ways a recognizably distinct minority within North African society). Perhaps things would have gone differently in Granada if Ibn Battuta had had a reputation as an outstanding scholar or Islamic lawyer rather than as a traveller. That in practical terms he was a competent and experienced judge, we may take for granted, but he was an observer, not a great thinker: there is no mention of either pious or legal studies written by him. Elsewhere on the margins of the Islamic world, as we have seen, he had the right kind of curriculum vitae to secure an entry into the halls of power, and often a lucrative appointment, but not in Granada.

Ibn Battuta's abilities as a powerful reporter could not be better illustrated than by the account he gives of an encounter he nearly had with Castilian Christian forces. This was a minor incident, the sort of thing that was occurring all the time on the kingdom's exposed Mediterranean coast. What happened to him was—nothing at all. Yet he manages to convey the intense feeling of imminent danger which he experienced. He achieves this with a basket of fish.

Travelling from Gibraltar, where he had landed, on towards Málaga, he passed through Marbella ('a pretty little town in a fertile district'—would that it had remained that way today!). There he met up with a troop of cavalry: 'and I wished to travel in their company', but the soldiers set off before him, unwilling to be encumbered by a civilian, we may suspect. Ibn Battuta followed them (presumably feeling safer if he followed at least as close behind as he could).

This is what he encountered just beyond the limits of Marbella:

I passed a dead horse lying in a ditch, and a little further on a pannier of fish thrown on the ground. This aroused my suspicions. In front of me was a watchtower, and I said to myself: 'If the enemy were to appear here, the man on the tower would give the alarm.' So I went forward to a house thereabouts, and at it I found a horse killed. While I was there I heard a shout behind me (for I had gone ahead of my party) and turning back to them, found the commander of the fort of Suhayl with them. He told me that four galleys belonging to the enemy had appeared there, and a number of the men on board had landed when the watchman was not in the tower. The horsemen who had just left Marbella, twelve in number, had encountered this raiding force. The Christians had killed one of them, one had escaped, and ten were taken prisoner. A fisherman was killed along with them, and it was he whose basket I had found lying on the road.

That is such an effective piece of writing because the terror is not directly present—it is just round the corner and may appear any moment—it is merely suggested. Will the marauding Christians rush out of the house? Or the watchtower? The master-stroke is that pannier of fish: an innocent thing itself, but inviting us to guess about the violence just a few minutes before that had caused it to be where it was. A skilled narrator is at work. And he is not Ibn Juzayy, who, if he had noticed the detail at all, would have capped it with a quotation from an apposite poem, by Ibn Khafaja perhaps. We shall never know exactly how much of the *Travels* is due to Ibn Juzayy, how much to Ibn Jubayr and other more remote sources, and how much by Ibn Battuta himself, but it would be absurd to seek to take away from 'the traveller *par excellence* of this our Muslim community' the credit for creating a work of art which so successfully evoked what he promised in his title, the *'aja'ib al-asfar*, the remarkable things he came across as he travelled.

Ibn Battuta has told us that he sailed from Ceuta to al-Andalus (Spain) because he 'wanted to take part in the holy war and the frontier fighting'. That still-fresh blood on the coast road from Marbella is the nearest he actually got to combat.

It would be totally unfair to blame a writer or his editor for not reporting some detail quite incidental to his subject, but since this chapter starts with a visit to Gibraltar, and since, with slightly puzzling chronology, our editor Ibn Juzayy (it surely must be he, and not Ibn Battuta) mentions being there at the time of the seige of Algeciras (in 1342), it is more than odd that there is no word concerning what, in the history of warfare, is most remarkable about that battle, the use of cannon: the first attested use of cannon in Europe. (The battle of Crécy in 1346 always gets a great deal of attention in this connection, presumably because Anglo-French conflicts are more familiar to many European historians.) Yet the fighting at Algeciras was a magnet attracting Christian participants from all over Western Europe, including, among many others, the Duke of Lancaster, or Earl of Derby as he then was, so news of the nature of the fighting might easily have reached England and France through this channel, or a dozen others. The innovative use of artillery at Algeciras, if mentioned at all, is often credited to the Castilians, presumably on the reasonable assumption that if the Castilians were ultimately victorious in this fighting, as they were, that was because of the superiority of their equipment. However, the Castilian chronicle[4] if read with attention, is quite unambiguous: the Muslim defenders, not the Christian attackers, were using, among other devices, *truenos* ('bombards', literally 'thunders'), a term not applicable to any of the mechanical, medieval engines for throwing projectiles). There is even the amusing detail that these bombards were so loud that across the bay in Gibraltar, reserve forces in the Muslim garrison, hearing all the noise, came to the mistaken conclusion that the final assault by the Christian besiegers had begun, and so a sortie from Gibraltar to relieve the embattled defenders of Algeciras was initiated. Nobody present then on either side could conceivably have been unaware of the unusually noisy weapons being tried out. Presumably Ibn Juzayy, who goes out of his way to tell us of his part in the combat, did not think such technical details worth bringing to our attention, or worthy of a place in literature (now if only a famous poet had composed verses on the subject, that would have been another matter). Ibn Battuta, coming on the scene not long after, devotes space to his inspection of the greatly enhanced defence works for Gibraltar constructed by Abu l-Hasan the Marinid. It would have been interesting to hear whether artillery as we know it was incorporated into these plans, and if not, why not. We are given an admiring description of the detailed scale model of Gibraltar which Abu l-Hasan had had constructed, and placed

---

[4]*Biblioteca de Autores Españoles*, lxvi. 359.

in his audience chamber in Fez to facilitate the study of the defence of the fortress. There is mention of 'magazines for munitions of war' but tantalizingly no indication whether these included guns and gunpowder.

SUFISM IN GRANADA

As we shall see (Chapter 10, p. 109), Ibn Battuta's extreme orthodox Maliki Sunni Islam, alongside his enthusiastic interest in Sufis and his ready acceptance of Sufi miracles, was a combination not always in line with what was to be found elsewhere in the Islamic world, where orthodox scholars and the Sufi cults could at times be at loggerheads. However, his native North Africa departed from the general pattern. Sunni orthodoxy in its Maliki form was securely predominant, but it coexisted with the cult of Sufi saints and holy men, particularly, but not exclusively, among the Berber tribes. So the yoking together in the *Travels* of these two aspects of Islam springs from what existed and was normal in the land in which he was born. In Spain the situation resembled that in North Africa, but was not identical to it. Malikism was in this relatively late period even more than predominant there, it was universal. And the society which produced one of the greatest Sufi divines of them all, Ibn al-'Arabi, was, of course, no stranger to Islamic mysticism. Nevertheless, as far as we can judge from the sources, Sufism failed to secure quite the same hold on society as it did in the East or in North Africa. The Nasrid dynasty had at the outset come to power in Granada in 1237 with a strong Sufi imprint, but it had been at pains to disengage itself from religious enthusiasts of dubious orthodoxy; the Nasrid sultans had prosecuted for heresy, and even executed, those who stirred up what were judged to be unhealthy religious movements.[5] Sufism had made some progress, but had not apparently the same secure base, in the craft guilds for example, as it had elsewhere. For these

[5]Harvey, *Islamic Spain*, 29–31.

reasons it is interesting to see what Ibn Battuta, with his worldwide experience in these matters, found worthy of note in this respect in Andalusia.

I also met in Granada the shaykh of the shaykhs and of the Sufis, the jurist Abu 'Ali 'Umar, son of the pious shaykh, the saint Abu 'Abdallah Muhammad b. al-Mahruq... I stayed for some days in his hospice outside Granada.

The 1929 version of this passage seems to me preferable:

I met...the principal Shaykh, who is also the superior of the Sufi orders.

Such espousal by one individual of the two aspects of the religion was, of course, by no means unknown elsewhere. Yet in Spain the orthodox seem to have been particularly successful in absorbing the Sufi movement (perhaps thus making it safe). Ibn Battuta mentions visiting two Sufi 'hospices', that of 'the Eagle' and that of 'the Bridle'.

The published English translations may mislead at this point. A tiny misprint in the full English translation places 'the Eagle' at eighty rather than eight miles from Granada (Vol. IV of the 1994 Hakluyt Society edition, p. 943), whereas Gibb in his 1929 selections (p. 316) has the distance correctly (the Arabic reads *nahw thamaniyya amyal*—approximately 12 rather than 120 kilometres). There can be no doubt about the sense: so small was this mountain kingdom that 120 kilometres in any direction would take one well beyond the boundaries of Muslim territory, so that cannot have been the original reading! As for 'the Bridle', the statement that it was 'at the top of the suburb of Najd outside Granada and adjoining Mount Sabika' is entirely correct, but will still convey to most readers a false impression. These Sufi centres were perched near to the seat of Nasrid power, and their location suggests that the movement was highly concentrated. Najd was a suburb outside the inner city limits, true, but it was in any perspective still very near indeed to the centre of things in Granada. The name Najd ('Uplands'), besides recalling the region of the

Arabian peninsula of that name, also reflects the fact that it was adjacent to the actual Alhambra hill (and 'Mount Sabika' is surely best translated in that way for English readers).

What is interesting for our present purposes is that (apart from the Granadan Abu 'Ali 'Umar already referred to, and he was a scholar, *'alim*, as well as a Sufi) those mystics mentioned by name are all outsiders: 'In Granada is a group of foreign faqirs [Gibb, 1929: 'Persian darwíshes']'. They were from Iran proper (Khorasan), Azerbayjan (Tabriz), Central Asia (Samarkand), Asia Minor (Konya), and India. Ibn Battuta finds no miracles of which to tell us on this short European excursion of his.

Where he finds Sufis, then, is in the capital city, and it is in part as an alien implant. This cannot be taken to indicate that these were the only Sufis, but they were the only ones he deemed worth reporting—a very different situation from what he finds elsewhere. We must beware of generalizing from such a short excursion, and from negative evidence, but elsewhere Ibn Battuta can usually be relied upon to track down the charismatic leaders of the popular local cults, and to tell us about them. In this aspect at least, his Spain is different.

From Gibraltar he crossed back to Ceuta, and went on to Asilah, Salé, Marrakesh, and thence, in the company of the Sultan, to Fez. Back in his native land, Ibn Battuta (or is it Ibn Juzayy?) becomes uncommunicative again. We are told nothing of his master's reaction to his journey to Granada, and nothing of the motives for his next great venture. If he had a mission entrusted to him, as he claims to have had when he went to the Far East from Delhi, we are told nothing of orders and instructions for this journey of his to the land of the Blacks. An apparently motiveless trek, probably the most dangerous journey he made, across the inhospitable Sahara, and eventually into pagan lands: is our traveller by now restlessly in pursuit of travel for its own sake, and not, as had been the case up to now, because of what he hoped to find when he arrived?

6

Africans

Ibn Battuta's experience of Africa outside Egypt was limited to two unconnected visits. The first was a fairly short voyage from Aden down the east coast of Africa, past the Horn of Africa (including Mogadishu), and as far as modern Tanzania (Kilwa appears to be the southernmost point he reached in the continent as a whole). The second, at the end of his travelling career, was a much more protracted trek by land across the Sahara and to the lands along the Niger, possibly as far south as the extreme north of modern Nigeria.

The long-established Islamic culture of what he calls the Sawahil country, the coastal belt of East Africa (where the mixed Swahili language was to arise out of trading contacts between Arab traders and Bantu speakers), had, of course, long enjoyed close cultural and religious links with Arabia. There may have been some exoticism in what he saw, facial tattoos, for example, but in general Ibn Battuta seems to have felt at home. There was prosperity, arising from the successful conduct of war by these principalities of the coast against the infidel tribes of the interior, but above all from the spice trade and other merchant ventures in the Indian Ocean. The Sultan of Kilwa, one Abu l-Muzaffar Hasan, 'was noted for his gifts and generosity... I have seen him give the clothes off his back to a mendicant who asked for them.' A ruler after Ibn Battuta's heart. The sultan's brother Dawud, however, who must have succeeded soon after Ibn Battuta left, did not come up to our traveller's approved standards of munificence: to a supplicant he is alleged to have said, 'He who gave is dead, and has left nothing behind to be given.'

From this land Ibn Battuta brought back no startling traveller's tales, nothing even to match what he claims he found at Zafar (Dhofar) when he got back to the Arabian peninsula: fish being used as fodder, 'the sole food of their beasts and flocks, a thing which I have seen nowhere else'.

The question of racial differences has somehow come to be seen in modern times as almost exclusively a matter of black versus white, or perhaps as black versus the rest. As he travelled the world Ibn Battuta observed differences between the peoples on his route, and provides us with fascinating ethnographic observations of all kinds, but he does not share the modern guilty preoccupation with negritude. This makes his reports of what he found in black and white Africa doubly interesting.

His explorations in sub-Saharan Africa came almost as a postscript, and after he had already established his reputation as a great traveller. In his journeys in North Africa and Eurasia, although he is often not able actively to choose his destinations, indeed he is at times a passive victim of fate, nevertheless it is possible to see in the background at all times the types of motivation which induced him to expose himself to all the vicissitudes of travel. He starts with the pious intention to make his pilgrimage to Makka and the other holy places, and there are associated journeys undertaken for purposes of study and edification. Ambition, never wholly absent as a motive, comes to the fore as he heads further east, and indeed in some places there it almost seems that it is not so much the pursuit of his career as a lawyer which predominates as expectation of personal gain, mingled with the dangerous game of politics at the highest level. What took him eastwards and then back home westwards is thus in some way comprehensible.

What of his expeditions southwards towards the heart of Africa?

Here the motives are less clear. Ibn Battuta did not stand to further his career by his perilous journeys, which had perforce to start with the crossing by some means or other of the land barrier presented by the Sahara desert. If he had some political mission entrusted to him there, as he tells us was the case when he set out from Delhi for Beijing, he tells us nothing about it. That gold dust (*tibr*) and refined gold (*dhahab*) had for centuries been brought north across the Sahara was common knowledge. Some 250 years after this exploration, a sultan of Morocco was successfully to mount an expedition that sent him back so much gold that he earned the epithet of 'the man of gold' (*al-Dhahabi:* Muley Ahmad al-Mansur), but there is no indication that greed for gold was the motive for Ibn Battuta. No, in the case of his explorations in the west of the African continent one feels that what drove him on into a very dangerous unknown was the need to cultivate and maintain that reputation as a traveller which he had gained in the Orient: this together with the underlying curiosity about the world which had been present from the beginning. For that reason what he is able to tell us is especially interesting. On this side of Africa his travels did not in fact take him very far beyond the lands into which Islam had already penetrated (and certainly not as far south as Tanzania on the eastern coast). He did see something of the interior of Africa, but this is not the 'opening up' of Africa: the rest of the world had to wait several hundred years more. What we see is the interface between the outer fringes of the truly Islamic lands (Dar al-Islam), and animistic Central Africa.

At the present day, in a world of racial tensions and colour conflicts, Muslims are rightly proud of the record of their religion in such matters. From the beginning, when the first muezzin entrusted with calling the faithful to prayer was Bilal, blacks have taken their full place alongside whites in the community (*umma*).

In Ibn Battuta's personal attitudes towards the African peoples amongst whom he travelled we find deep contradictions. The blacks, in his eyes, 'possess admirable qualities. They are seldom unjust, and have a greater abhorrence of injustice than any other people'.

(Let us not forget that it is a professional judge who is making this observation.) 'Their sultan shows no mercy to anyone who is guilty of the least unjust act', he tells us.

There is complete security in their country. Neither traveller nor inhabitant in it has anything to fear from robbers or men of violence. They do not confiscate the property of any white man who dies in their country, even if it is uncounted wealth. On the contrary, they give it into the charge of some trustworthy person among the whites, until the rightful heir takes possession of it. Their mosques are crowded. And they are clean: on Fridays, 'even if a man has nothing but an old worn shirt, he washes it and cleans it and wears it to the Friday service.'

It will be clear from the above passage that it is describing the state of affairs in the lands on the bend of the Niger where Islam had already penetrated, not in territories further south where peoples were still pagan.

Can we then say that Ibn Battuta himself was devoid of racial prejudice? There are several passages which would certainly be in danger nowadays of being taken as a clear indication of contempt for blacks. The impact of the following episode becomes no less shocking if we bear in mind that the 'blacks' in question may have been of mixed blood. (Ibn Battuta may have been misled by the use of indigo pigmentation by the 'white' desert Berbers.) At Iwalatan (Walata, Oualata) at the end of an arduous two-month trek across the Sahara from Sijilmassa, the merchants with whom Ibn Battuta travelled were summoned/invited to call on the Sultan's deputy, Farbá Husayn. As Ibn Battuta describes it, Farbá Husayn made a parade of his guards, and then addressed the newly arrived traders 'through an interpreter, although they were close to him, to show his contempt for them.' (This is an example of Ibn Battuta failing to understand the local customs. What Ibn Battuta interpreted as 'contempt' was no more than established protocol.) 'It was then that I repented of having come to their country,' he confesses *because of their lack of manners, and their contempt for the whites*' (emphasis added, but his exact words). He had the same hostile reaction when another local dignitary, the inspector Manshú Jú, invited the whole caravan in which Ibn Battuta had arrived to 'partake of his hospitality'. What he offered was 'some pounded millet mixed with a little honey and milk, put in a half calabash shaped like a large bowl.' 'Was it for this that the black invited us?', Ibn Battuta muttered to his companions. When told that this was their highest form of hospitality, he became convinced 'that there was no good to be hoped from these people'. It might, I suppose be possible to argue that 'black' in the passages just cited is purely and objectively descriptive, and that Ibn Battuta's obvious prejudice was a negative reaction to his hosts' extreme poverty or meanness, rather than against their race. Accustomed as he had become to the lavish receptions accorded in Delhi and elsewhere to such as him, his disappointed greed led him to write off this distant spot as unlikely to bring him profit: 'I made up my mind to travel [back at once] with the pilgrim caravan from Iwalatan'. It would seem to me, however, that the incident does uncover a side of Ibn Battuta's character somewhat more unpleasant than his greed (and of course we can be in no doubt about that after what he tells us about his travels in India and the Maldive Islands). It is in terms of colour conflict ('their lack of manners and their contempt for the whites') that he interprets the behaviour of the local people towards him, and it seems reasonable to interpret his own responses to them in the same way.

In his travels in this region, Ibn Battuta normally identifies the people he comes across by colour: 'Ten days after leaving Iwalatan we came to the village of Zaghari, a large village inhabited by negro traders called *wanjarata*, along with whom live a community of whites of the Ibadite sect.' (The Ibadis are said to be—though they themselves dispute this—a remnant of the Kharijis who, in the early days of Islam, sought a refuge for their beliefs, heretical in the eyes of Sunni orthodoxy, in distant desert locations beyond the bounds of normal habitation.)

It has to be said in this connection that in the book as a whole, the people for whom Ibn Battuta reserves his most disparaging remarks are not Africans, they are the white, blue-eyed Europeans he claims to have encountered in what we would call the Ukraine: he calls them Russians. Not that he claimed to have travelled in their land. When passing along the shore of the Sea of Azov, and in speaking of the 'extremely cold' town of Ukak, (probably a port on its northern shore), he remarks: 'A day's march from this town are the mountains of the Russians. These are Christians, red-haired and blue-eyed, with ugly faces and treacherous.' Christians from regions outside the Middle East seem to have evoked a similar reaction. In his account of Constantinople, he tells us that 'The second part, on the western bank of the river [Bosphorus] is called Galata, and is reserved to the Frankish Christians who dwell there. They are of different kinds, including Genoese, Venetians, Romans, and people of France.' He is impressed by the shipping he sees, and the bazaars, 'good but filthy, and a small and very dirty river runs through them. Their churches too are filthy and mean.'

The foreigner then, and particularly the non-Muslim foreigner from outside those parts of the world where standards of hygiene could be set by Islamic rulers, was lacking in cleanliness. We learn relatively little of such people, for Ibn Battuta the Islamic scholar seems to have avoided contact with them if he could (see Chapter 5). But the black Africans, with that distressing habit of theirs, on which he remarks, of scattering dust over their head as a sign of respect, were certainly placed by him in a lower category than pagans such as the Hindus in India or the Chinese. The masks and costumes of the tribal bards (*griots* is the word usually employed nowadays in the ethnographic literature, but the word he uses is *jali*) at the court of Mansa Sulayman, the Sultan of Malli are simply derided: 'Each of them is inside a costume made of feathers resembling a green woodpecker, on which is a wooden head with a red beak, like the head of a woodpecker. They stand before the Sultan in this laughable get-up, and recite their poems.'

Black Muslims are praised for their punctilious observance of religious obligations, and for the stress they place on memorizing the Qur'an, but even in this context the anecdote he tells is an odd one: 'One day I passed by a handsome youth, who was very well dressed, with a heavy shackle on his foot. I said to the person with me: "What has he done? Has he killed someone?" The youth understood what I said, and laughed. I was told: 'He has been shackled to make him memorize the Qur'an." '

As in the Maldive Islands, female nakedness Ibn Battuta found particularly difficult to accept where Muslims were concerned (see Chapter 9, p. 112): 'On the night of the twenty-seventh of Ramadan I have seen about a hundred naked slave-girls come out of his [i.e. the Mansa Sulayman's] palace with food: with them were two daughters of the Sultan with full breasts, and they too had no veil.'

What really horrifies Ibn Battuta is cannibalism (the practice of 'infidels who eat the sons of Adam'). If we are to believe one of Ibn Battuta's anecdotes, cannibalism must still have existed in border territories subject to the Sultan of Malli. To punish an unsatisfactory white qadi caught peculating, the Sultan had had him posted in cannibal territory, but then brought him back after four years: 'The infidels had not eaten him because he was white, for they say that eating a white man is harmful because he is "unripe". They claim that a black is "ripe".'

More startling still is the following story, which if genuine implies active complicity between Muslim ruler and pagan subjects:

A group of these blacks came to Sultan Mansa Sulaiman with their emir. It is their custom to put in their ears big pendants half a span across. They wrap themselves in silk, and in their country is a gold mine. The Sultan received them with honour and gave them in hospitality a slave woman, whom they killed and ate. They smeared their faces and hands with her blood, and came to the Sultan to thank him. I was told that this is their custom whenever they come on an embassy to him. It was reported of them that they used to say that the best parts of the flesh of human females were the palm of the hand and the breast.

After reading such anecdotes, accounts of plain consumption of carrion meat seem tame: 'The camel I was riding died...I went out to look at it, and found that the blacks had already eaten it in accordance with their practice of eating carrion.'

The attitudes taken by modern commentators towards these reports vary a great deal. On the one hand, as seen by Said Hamdun and Noël King, who were writing,[1] primarily for an educated African readership, it was all a joke at the outsider's expense that Ibn Battuta failed to understand: 'It is amazing how ingenuous and gullible this experienced traveller can be.' The atrocities are 'excellent stories to prove white men are both immature and dishonest, both told with obvious gusto and laughter by his sophisticated African informant.' In contrast Gibb and Beckingham (and I think at this point we can assume the annotation is by Beckingham) appear to take the information at its face value, and even add an extra cannibal story for good measure. The note reads: 'The head-hunting and cannibal tribes are located in the central pagan belt extending from Yola to the confines of Zaria province (C. K. Meek, *The Northern Tribes of Nigeria*, 1925, 11, p. 48).' Thirty-four cannibal tribes are listed, and the same author notes that among the non-cannibal peoples we find many traces of former cannibal customs. It is related by al-'Omari that a merchant gave some salt to a pagan king of the Blacks, and in return was sent two young women for him to eat.'[2] It is easy to determine which of the two approaches is likely to be adjudged the more 'politically correct', but I am quite unable to determine which in this context is likely to be nearer to the truth of the matter. One thing is clear, however, and that is that Ibn Battuta did not himself invent the stories of this type.

Hamdun and King even manage to dispose of the carrion camel story. The offence, they imply, was not lack of respect for the *halal* regulations, but theft. 'Later, when some people make a meal of his camel, they tell him it had died, [and] he rushes out to find they have already eaten it. His only emotion is disgust at their eating a dead animal.' Hamdun and King may well be right here, but I do not see how we can be sure.

[1] *Ibn Battuta in Black Africa* (Princeton, NJ: Markus Wiener Publishers, 2nd edn., 1994), 92.
[2] *The Travels of Ibn Battuta* AD *1325–1354* (London: The Hakluyt Society, 1994), iv. 968, n. 73.

One may perhaps infer from Ibn Battuta's only reported spiritual experience in this part of the world—it was in the town where he had had his camel eaten—that he had become profoundly disturbed.

One night while I was staying in this town, I saw in my sleep a person who said to me: 'O Muhammad ibn Battuta, why do you not recite the sura *Ya-Sin* every night?' Since then I have not failed to recite it daily, whether I have been travelling or not.

Ya-Sin is the sura that in many parts of the Islamic world the pious recite on behalf of the dead; it is also widely read by Muslims in order to bring security from situations of danger.

PART THREE

Themes

7

Finance and the *Travels*

FINANCE

A constant theme in Ibn Battuta's writing is the hospitality which he received, and the numerous financial subventions and gifts of quite startling generosity that were showered on him, both by his hosts and by people he encountered by chance along his way. To estimate his total income from such sources while he was on his travels would be quite impossible: some of the bounty he received can only be guessed at very approximately (what would the capital value be of the income from certain Indian villages for unspecified lengths of time?). We do have details of a surprising number of his transactions, but certainly nothing approaching a complete record.

Curiously he tells us nothing of his financial circumstances when he started out on his travels. A young man of 22, hardly more than a student, he must have received substantial help from his family to enable him to begin his journeying, for although a pilgrim to the holy places, he did not travel as a pauper. At a very early stage (when he had gone no further than Sfax in present-day Tunisia) we find him already contemplating marriage to a wellborn young lady from Tunis, then, after that match had fallen through, he did get married to 'the daughter of a student from Fez', and entertained the entire caravan with which he was travelling at his wedding reception. Even if we assume that the bride-price of the girl from Fez was more modest than that of the young lady from Tunis would have been, all this speaks of a young man not devoid of means. He had already begun to receive alms from the pious. In Constantine (in present-day Algeria) the city governor, observing that Ibn Battuta had got soaked by the rain in the mountains, not only had his clothes laundered and dried for him, but in place of his worn old headcloth *(ihram,* the word used, more generally has the sense of the pilgrim's seamless robe, but here presumably it has its Western Arabic meaning of 'head covering'), presented him with a new one in Syrian cloth, and into it slipped two dinars. This, as he tells us, was the first alms of his journey.

As the caravan advanced towards Makka, he continued to be given alms of moderate amounts. Near Alexandria, when he visited the Shaykh al-Murshidi (a visit of great importance in the structure of the book: see Chapter 2) he was given a travel-provision of small cakes and money. Shortly after leaving Damietta, a horseman sent out by the governor caught up with him, and handed over 'a number of coins'.

And so it went on: small-scale generosity, appropriate and welcome assistance, but not at this stage great riches. His fortunes began to turn in Damascus, where a local Maliki professor, Nur al-Din Sakhawi, hired for him camels to take him across the gruelling next stages of the Arabian desert, and gave him money as well, saying, 'It will come in for any serious matter that may land you in difficulties.' By the time his pilgrimage to Makka itself was completed, Ibn Battuta was already enjoying powerful patronage: 'On the 17 May I left Makka with the commander of the 'Iraq caravan, who hired for me at his own expense the half of a camel litter as far as Baghdad, and took me under his protection.'

Thus far Ibn Battuta's movements were within the framework of the Makkan pilgrimage. (And it was by no means unusual for someone who had made the pilgrimage to the holy places to go on as he was doing to visit other parts of the east for purposes of study and edification.) It was when Ibn Battuta turned from

Iraq into the mountains of Luristan that there emerged the first intimation of a pattern that was eventually to predominate through the rest of his wanderings, although after Luristan he at first returned to cycles of Makkan-centred travels through the Middle East. The new pattern was that, thanks to his growing reputation as a traveller, he was able to finance his travels: by narrating the journeys he had already completed he could earn his supper on his way to his next destination.

His journey to Luristan was taken at the prompting of an unidentified man from Basra, and at the outset we are told nothing of Ibn Battuta's motive for following that route. Beyond Tustar (Shushtar) in Khuzestan he ascended into the mountains (the Zagros range) and at Mal al-Amir (near Shushtar) he reached the court of the Atabeg, which as he explains, was 'a title common to all the rulers of that country'. Here the Atabeg kept him waiting at first, but after a few days Ibn Battuta was admitted into the ruler's presence, in the company of the chamberlain and one of the 'boon-companions'.

There are two elements in this interview, and they are elements we find consistently throughout the rest of Ibn Battuta's writings. In part of the interview, Ibn Battuta recounted to the ruler tales of distant lands. The sultan sat on a cushion 'with two covered goblets in front of him one of gold and the other of silver' and asked about 'myself and my country, the sultan of Egypt and the Hijaz.' The other element shows us Ibn Battuta the religious teacher and preacher. When one of the court, a 'noted doctor of the law', came in and joined the circle, it soon became clear he was very drunk, and so Ibn Battuta did not fail to point out the evils of wine before he withdrew (the Atabeg himself by now was 'reeling and on the point of failing asleep'). In one of the little touches that help to convince us that we are being told about something which really happened, Ibn Battuta, once outside, tells us he discovered that he had forgotten to bring his sandals out with him when he left, and he is rather ashamed of himself when it is the bibulous 'doctor of the law' who offers to go in and rescue them.

'A few days later I left...and the sultan sent me a number of dinars as a farewell gift, and a like sum for my companions.' What is more they were all enabled to make use of well-appointed hospices and colleges as they made their way on to Isfahan. The sum of money may not have been large, but Ibn Battuta was launched on his new career in which he combined narrating his travels with the exercise of his profession as lawyer. Up to this stage he had gone to places because they were on his road. He might meet men of importance, but that was incidental. In Luristan, however, he says 'I wished to see the sultan'.

Ibn Battuta now had the confidence and contacts required to secure the entrée to royal courts in this way. In Baghdad and elsewhere in Iraq he travelled for some time with the camp of the Ilkhan (he was to be last of the line) Abu Sa'id Bahadur Khan, and was at last rewarded by being summoned into the royal presence: 'The sultan asked me about my country, and gave me a robe and a horse.' (Such a robe, of course, would be a costly ceremonial garment.) What is more, he could usually expect to be accorded official hospitality while crossing the territory administered by the ruler in question. After his successful interview with Abu Sa'id Bahadur Khan, for example, one of the sultan's emirs 'gave orders for me to be supplied with provisions and to travel with the cortege of the commander of the pilgrim caravan, and wrote instructions to that effect to the governor of Baghdad'— which assistance Ibn Battuta acknowledges he received 'in full'. From Baghdad onwards, the governor had assigned to this young scholar 'half a camel litter and provisions and water for four persons', but in fact 'he gave me even more than had been ordered for me.' One begins to see how it was possible for these great journeys to be made. One could travel and not only have one's expenses covered: one could actually save money along the way.

There are two stories told by Ibn Battuta which indicate that the simple and basic financial relationship between pilgrim/traveller and patron/ruler at times became quite complicated, and subject to what the modern speculative financial advisor might call 'gearing', so that the financial transactions were sufficiently profitable to attract the attentions of brokers and loan sharks.

The first story concerns a matter of the speculative advance of funds in pursuit of personal profit: we may think it foolish of Ibn Battuta to get involved in such transactions, but no doubt he felt he had to conform to the customs of the country in which he found himself. It was much to Ibn Battuta's potential advantage that the ruler of Delhi, Sultan Muhammad ibn Tughluq, preferred to bestow his favours on foreigners. However, 'every person proceeding to the court of this king must have a gift ready to present to him, in order to gain his favour. Although the sultan could be relied upon to return a gift many times the value of what was given, there was the initial outlay to find, the problem of raising the cash to buy a gift fit for a king in the first place. Merchants in Sind and India saw the chance to develop a business in loans, and to put up the cash ('thousands of dinars') 'to supply him with whatever he might desire to offer as a gift, or to use on his own behalf'. After the audience with the ruler, the expectation was that the loan would be paid off: 'This trade of theirs is a flourishing one, and brings in vast profits.' Ibn Battuta raised a loan, first from an Iraqi merchant in Ghazna ('thirty horses and a camel with a load of arrows'), but then in Sind, finding the credit so easy to obtain, adds horses, camels, white slaves and other goods. No doubt the outlay was justified, when eventually Ibn Battuta reached court, even before he had his actual audience with the Sultan, he had bounty showered on him. At the outset he was given 'two purses each containing 1,000 silver dinars' with the message: 'This is for washing your head.' And all members of Ibn Battuta's numerous household participated in his fortune: 200 dinars each for 'companions', 150 and 100 for the middle ranks, 65 for slave boys, and so on, to a total of 4,000-odd dinars! Besides the gifts in money came those in kind, a daily allowance of 1,000 pounds of flour, 1,000 pounds of meat, and others. 'Later on the sultan commanded some villages to be assigned to me to the yearly revenue of 5,000 dinars.' One might suspect that this was pure boastful fantasy on Ibn Battuta's part, but although no doubt the story has not lost anything in the telling, all the same this Sultan's extraordinary generosity to his visitors, particularly to his foreign visitors, is amply attested in the record.

The financial sophistication of this loan-finance scheme operated for private gain was matched by the system of paper credit for vows and alms. Ibn Battuta tells us how he himself helped operate such a system on the junk bringing him back from the South China coast. Somewhere out on the high seas (they had been lost for forty-two days, and had no idea where they were) panic struck. They thought they were about to be shipwrecked on a precipitous island. The merchants on board began to pray, and on the spot, there and then on the ship, began to issue promissory notes to distribute alms in the future (in order to establish spiritual credit in the present). 'I wrote down their vows for them in a register with my own hand,' Ibn Battuta tells us. This was not a unique occurrence, indeed we learn elsewhere in the *Travels* of the existence of brokers specialized in the market of redeeming such 'futures'.

If the first stage of Ibn Battuta's travels saw him glad to be given two dinars, he then became accustomed to favoured treatment in the caravans. By the time he was in Luristan heading eastwards he had established his reputation as a successful narrator of travels to princes, and as a kind of professional entertainer. Delhi was the high point. To the generous hospitality gifts, can be added the emoluments of the office of Maliki qadi. It can hardly be said that from then onwards the trend was downhill, for, if we are to believe him, he continued to enjoy favours. Good fortune continued, but not unabated.

There came a point in his travels when Ibn Battuta sought to add to the income he received from the practice of law (a safe living, but the rewards were modest) and from his life as a courtier (which might bring dazzling rewards, but which as a way of life was devoid of security, and downright dangerous at times) by actively going out to make money as an entrepreneur. Perhaps one might say as a currency speculator. That is a sensational term to use, and the reader must judge whether it is justified. Ibn Battuta went into cowrie shells.

One still finds nowadays, in the ethnographic literature relating to various parts of the world, that these tiny shells are used as a medium of exchange, part ornament but basically currency. In the Maldives Ibn Battuta was in one of the favoured centres of production of this exchange token. He must have decided to take advantage of the situation in which he found himself.

He tells us about the production process: 'This is a creature they gather from the sea, and then place in pits, where its flesh rots away, leaving the white shell'. We may note that no heavy capital outlay was required. The wide range of exchange rates for this form of money as reported by Ibn Battuta signals enormous potential commercial opportunities for the primary producers: the standard rate was 400,000 shells to a gold dinar, but frequently it would fall to 1,000,000 to a dinar (at that rate one finds oneself wondering whether the shells would have been worth processing). Cowries were in use as currency in Bengal; later Ibn Battuta was to find them valued at 1,150 to the dinar in Africa on the bend of the Niger. These are the extreme values mentioned by him. There is no suggestion that Ibn Battuta tried to trade them from the Maldives directly to Africa. (If he could have brought that off, it would indeed have been a profitable venture!) He did go in for export from the islands to India, but he ran into opposition from the Maldivian authorities.

We have only Ibn Battuta's by no means complete account of what lay behind this opposition to his dealing in shells, but it is very probable that it arose as a consequence of the annoyance he had caused by accepting very generous presents from the vizier of the islands in consideration of a promise to marry, on which he reneged. After going back on the agreement, Ibn Battuta continued with his plans to trade in cowries, while planning to move away from the islands to India. (One can imagine the disastrous effect it would have had on the Maldivian economy if he had dumped his cargo of shells on their principal market.) 'If you wish to go, give us back what we have given you,' he was told. He had to reply that some of the jewels presented to him had been used to buy cowries. And so he offered to hand over the cowries instead. 'We gave you gold, not cowries,' he was reminded. Ibn Battuta tried to get himself out of the fix by offering to sell back the cowries. That, not surprisingly, was not permitted. Ibn Battuta's explanation for this impasse was the one, flattering to himself, that his presence in the islands was so valued that they did not want him to go. A compromise was found: Ibn Battuta was to stay, but was to be allowed to sell off his cowries in Bengal using an agent of his own, who was to be 'aided' by someone sent by the Maldivians: al-Hajj 'Ali. In fact the business venture must have failed completely, for the boat Ibn Battuta had bought to take his precious cargo to Bengal ran into such a bad storm that, in order to lighten ship, those on board threw absolutely everything they had overboard, even water and provisions. The vessel drifted, dismasted and rudderless, for sixteen nights, and eventually reached Ceylon. Ibn Battuta does not analyze for us his disastrous venture, that was not his way, but he must have regretted an unwise speculation that turned out so badly. One can well understand, then, the way he envied a man he came across at this stage in his travels on one of the tiny outer islands. This man was a weaver, and he had just a few coconut palms, banana plants, and what he could fish from the sea to sustain him and his family: 'I swear I envied that man, and wished that the island were mine, to make of it a retreat until the Last Hour comes.'

Needless to say, our traveller did not succumb to that desire, and as we know, he continued his journeying. Ibn Battuta had created for himself a way of financing his perpetual motion: what was impossible for him was to settle down for more than a few years. Whether outside the cash economy (as the weaver virtually was) or inside it, he would always feel the need to move on. In the Maldives he was clearly happy and well-to-do, but he was still driven to leave. Financial considerations were never ignored by Ibn Battuta—his book makes it clear that they were never far from his thoughts—but what drove him ever onwards was something else.

One of the practicalities of moving about the world that is often shrouded by taboos in any period of history is the vital question of travel expenses. 'How much did it cost?' may not be a question that produces very interesting answers if we do not have a feel for the value of the coinage in use (and we rarely do), but 'Where did he actually get the money from?' almost invariably does tell us a great deal. Did the traveller start out with resources for the whole journey, did he have money remitted to him (and how), or did he acquire it along the way? In Ibn Battuta's case such information is not consistently supplied, but we are given more in the way of detail than is found in many coy travel narratives.

Ibn Battuta, who at the end became, I suggest, a traveller for travelling's sake, started out with very different motivation, and several advantages. In the first place, during the first leg of his journeying, from North Africa westwards, he was performing the Islamic pilgrimage, and he could legitimately benefit from that great network of administrative arrangements and pious benefactions which had been built up over the centuries in support of pilgrims. In the second place, the associated institution of travel in pursuit of Islamic learning meant that there was available to him a socially-approved role. The modern Western traveller, in some parts of the world, where no such approved role exists, is sometimes hard put to it to overcome the suspicions of the peoples among whom he moves. What does this strange stranger want here? Does he represent some form of threat?

For so long as he stayed within the bounds of the Islamic world, Ibn Battuta had little need to explain himself: as a young scholar ('*alim*), everybody understood his need to seek out distant sources of Islamic learning and wisdom. And as the very well-known Arabic expression had it, such learning had to be hunted out 'even in China'. The wording would be taken in most cases as figure of speech, an exaggeration, intended to hammer the point home that learning was not to be had if one was not prepared to bestir oneself to obtain it; but in the face of that well-known phrase, who could question the appropriateness of a religious scholar taking to the roads and heading eastwards? In contrast, the wandering scholar clerics who were Ibn Battuta's exact contemporaries in medieval Europe ran the risk of being condemned as goliards, and of being drawn into a sub-culture of 'truancy' (as some have called it), free to celebrate wine, women, and song—until a worthwhile ecclesiastical benefice came their way. For the university educated, it would seem that the job market in the East was more buoyant than in the West, and more advantageously arranged. Travel for the Islamic scholar was not an escape from social commitment, as it might be in the case of the goliards, it was often a quite necessary phase on the road to advancement.

Ibn Battuta, who started his travels as a young scholar, had nevertheless completed enough formal law study, before he set out, to qualify him to begin to practise his profession in the lands he visited. (No doubt the fact that he came from a family of distinguished lawyers gave him a flying start.) In this connection he was eventually helped by the eagerness shown by the rulers of some Islamic lands far removed from the established centres of Islamic scholarship to recruit and retain the services of scholars. The pious motive of providing Muslims with proper legal services was what led to such recruitment, but one does not have to be a cynic to recognize that present too was the competitive pursuit of prestige. These were factors working to the advantage of young lawyers in search of advancement. Ibn Battuta was fortunate to be somebody with the right qualifications at the right time and place. Once he had established a reputation for himself, travel could in some places be lucrative. He is almost shamefaced at times when he comes to speak of the splendid *train de vie* that he could afford, his many servants and slaves, his string of horses.

Then once he had gained experience as a lawyer in responsible positions, especially after serving as Maliki qadi in Delhi the way was opened for him to begin a second career as a diplomat. Here again circumstances favoured him in a number of ways. In many periods and countries people who began as outsiders have been able to climb to the top as representatives of the interests of their adopted country (a recent example might be the career of Henry Kissinger in the USA, but there were many others in the nineteenth century and earlier). In Ibn Battuta's world, where the very concepts of nationality and citizenship do not apply, there was certainly no bar against the employment of outsiders as emissaries. There was demand: the great powers of the day all needed diplomats, but in addition many quite small states for reasons of prestige had their envoys. For the services of skilled and experienced men like Ibn Battuta there was competition. The job market worked in his favour.

Also working in his favour were the conventional conditions of service of emissaries and ambassadors. In our days we take it for granted that an ambassador will be paid by the government sending him. If he were to be given gifts, he would expect to inform his home government, who would certainly regard any regular payments as more than suspicious. It would be assumed that he had been 'turned', and was working for the other side. In Ibn Battuta's world, things were done differently. The emissary expected, as a guest, to be lodged and fed by the host government, and it is clear from Ibn Battuta's remarks that if the host were not generous, the emissary adjudged himself unfortunate. Once Ibn Battuta had passed beyond the status of wandering scholar and entered upon the linked careers of, first, Islamic lawyer and then diplomat, travel became not just something which he could do with a reasonable hope that he would be charitably lodged and fed, but also an activity which could bring him real wealth. It is true that it was not without its dangers too: highway robbers, pirates, and even hired assassins, floods, fires, and pestilences. But for the adventurous this was a period of open horizons. Ibn Battuta knew great good fortune at times, and at times hardship and worse, but the good times outnumbered the bad. Far from home, he usually was nevertheless in no doubt about the source of his next meal. Quite often that meal was a refined banquet served to him in a state guest-house.

8

Natural history

The modern traveller seems sometimes to be undertaking his travel-pilgrimage simply in order to worship at the shrine of wild nature, and to accumulate merit by observing as many species as possible. Animals do not occupy a very high station in Ibn Battuta's list of priorities, but where he comes across something unusual, particularly where an animal is reckoned as one of the remarkable things (*'aja'ib*) of the region in question, he gives details (although he never allows animals to threaten to oust humans from his narrative). We will see that some of the tales he has to tell are not credible, but it is remarkable how many of his descriptions, unlike those given by his contemporaries, are borne out by modern zoological observations.

The Elephant

We might at first be inclined to take the story of the elephants and the imam 'Abdallah ibn Khafif ('the Shaykh') as just one more of the many improbable miracle stories associated with holy men at this period. 'Abdallah, a spiritual leader, originally from Shiraz in Iran, clearly made a considerable impression on Ibn Battuta. With thirty of his devout followers he had set out on a pilgrimage to the crest of Adam's Peak in Ceylon. The thirty were overcome with hunger on the way up, and against their Shaykh's explicit orders, assuaged it by catching and eating a baby elephant! They offered some of the meat to him, but he refused it. That night elephants gathered as the party slept, and sniffed out each one of the thirty who had partaken of elephant flesh, and killed him. As for the Shaykh, they not only did not harm him: one of them lifted him onto his back with his trunk, and carried the exhausted old man back to where there were some people. 'As it came near them, the elephant lifted him with its trunk and placed him on the ground in full view of them.' The picture which is presented of the herd, and the way it relied so largely on the power of scent, so that it was able to pick out 'Abdallah ibn Khafif from among his guilty companions, and to convey him to safety, certainly seems remarkable, but not altogether impossible. It is well attested that herds of elephants may display respect and apparent intense grief over the remains of dead members of their family.

The elephant for Ibn Battuta is no menagerie amusement or cosy jumbo providing rides for children. For him the beast is a creature of immense power and danger. He tells of one despot, Muhammad ibn Tughluq, using elephants as a means of executing his prisoners.

These elephants which kill men have their tusks fitted with pointed blades of iron resembling ploughshares, with edges like knives. The mahout mounts on the elephant, and when a man is thrown before it, it winds its trunk around him, throws him in the air, then catches him with its tusks and throws him after that at its feet, places one foot upon his chest and does with him what the mahout orders him to do in accordance with the Sultan's commands to him. If he orders him to be left alone it leaves him lying on the ground and he is flayed. It was this punishment which was inflicted on those amirs, and when I came out of the Sultan's encampment at sunset I saw the dogs eating their flesh, their skins having been stuffed with straw—God preserve us.

In the city of Zihar (Dhar) in central India the vizier Khwaja Jahan had a member of his family put to death for rebellion and attempted assassination by throwing him to the elephants in a similar way.

Ibn Battuta has nothing to say of the difference between the Indian and African species, which is disappointing. His travels in sub-Saharan Africa to Timbuktu and beyond took him into the zone which, still today, in spite of the advance of the desert and the retreat of the sort of vegetation on which elephants depend, is visited by these animals. In the fourteenth century African elephants must have been much more numerous, and it will be seen in the next section that he was aware of their existence, but he says nothing of their distinctive appearance or habits.

The Hippopotamus

From the same general area, in modern Mali on the Niger, he reports what was his first sighting, of the hippopotamus. It was by night: the mosquitoes thereabouts were so thick that by day travel was not possible (of that more below).

We reached the channel [of the Niger] three or four hours after nightfall on a moonlit night. On reaching it I saw sixteen beasts with enormous bodies, and marvelled at them, taking them to be elephants, of which there are many in that country. Afterwards I saw that they had gone into the river, so I said to Abu Bakr, 'What kind of animals are those?' He replied, 'They are hippopotamuses which have to come out to graze on land.' They are bulkier than horses, have manes and tails, and their heads are like horses' heads, but their feet are like elephants' feet. I saw these hippopotamuses again when we sailed down the [Niger] from Tumbuktu to Gawgaw [Gao]. They were swimming in the water, and lifting their heads and blowing. The men in the boat were afraid of them, and kept close to the bank in case the hippopotamuses should sink them.

All that, including especially the reference to the habit of coming ashore to graze by night, is more likely to be a direct observation than to be derived from a written source (accurate early descriptions of the habits of the hippopotamus do not abound). But what of the horse's head (just possibly a rough approximation), and in particular the mane? Had perhaps the hippopotamuses Ibn Battuta saw covered themselves with mud, so that it was difficult to see details of their heads at night?

The Rhinoceros

On the rhinoceros there are no details at all, although Ibn Battuta places them accurately in the right environment (for his day), and one has no reason to doubt him. 'After crossing the river of Sind called Panj Ab, our way led through a forest of reeds, in which I saw a rhinoceros for the first time.' Presumably in Africa he did not penetrate far enough south to see any at all.

Hyenas

In Upper Egypt, after visiting Luxor, out in the open desert, one halt was at

Humaythira, a place infested with hyenas. All night long we kept driving them away, and indeed one got at my baggage, tore open one of the sacks, pulled out a bag of dates, and made off with it. We found the bag next morning torn to pieces, and with most of the contents eaten.

Monkeys

The 'vast numbers' of monkeys of Ceylon are noted by Ibn Battuta, particularly the *Macaca silenus*, of which the males are 'bearded like men'. What he fastened on were the human-like aspects of their social system, and, a subject never far from this traveller's mind, their sexual behaviour. He observes the power of the dominant male, and conceptualizes this as being on the lines of the human interactions of a petty court. The dominant male was the 'Sultan', as he puts it, with the subdominants (he tells us there were four) in attendance on him, and food (banana, orange, some such fruit) being taken from those of inferior status and enjoyed by the dominants, while those who stepped out of line were beaten mercilessly by the inner circle. No doubt Ibn Battuta was familiar with such a social set-up. He plays up the humanoid aspects: the chief monkey 'leans upon a staff' and wears a garland of leaves, but it was the potential sexual threat stemming from all this animal activity that fascinated him. He tells a story, carefully pointing out that he had it at second hand, from 'trustworthy persons'. 'When one of these monkeys seizes a girl who is unable to defend herself, he has intercourse with her.' And more specifically:

I was told by one of the inhabitants of this island that there was in his house a monkey of this kind, one of his daughters went into a chamber, and the animal followed her in, and though she screamed at it, it got the better of her, and he added: 'When we came into the room after her, it was between her legs and so we killed it.'

Leeches

In these same tropical forests of the interior of Ceylon, Ibn Battuta was plagued by leeches. He observes, very soundly, that they were to be found in trees and vegetation near water, and gives helpful practical advice on how to cause those which have attached themselves to one's flesh to release their grip (by applying salt and lemon). He must have been puzzled by the ability of these infuriating creatures to find their target, and he tells us that this was because 'when a man approaches it jumps out at him, and wheresoever it alights on his body, the blood flows.' So they were flying leeches, which they call *zulu*! It is curious that although he gives such good advice on one jungle pest, the leech, the advice he has on mosquitoes is totally wrong. As we saw above under 'Hippopotamus', he tells us that they are active by day and not by night, the reverse of the truth.

Crocodiles

I saw a crocodile [in the Niger], close to the bank; it looked just like a small boat. One day I went down to the river to satisfy a need, and lo, one of the blacks came and stood between me and the river. I was amazed at such lack of manners and decency on his part, and spoke of it to someone or other. He answered 'His purpose in doing that was solely to protect you from the crocodile, by placing himself between you and it.'

One admires in this anecdote Ibn Battuta's honest admission of his own prejudices. He jumps to the conclusion that it is the black who is lacking in manners and decency (we have seen that would be in line with his general opinion as expressed elsewhere), and it is only in retrospect that he realizes he had misread the situation totally, and that in a gratuitous act of kindness the man had been protecting him from a very real danger.

Tigers

At 'Parven' (identified with some probability as Narwar in Gwalior state), one of the inhabitants told Ibn Battuta that a 'tiger' (Arabic *sab*', perhaps a leopard) used to enter the town by night, even though the gates were closed, and seize people, and carried off a boy who had been lying on his bed in this informant's house. The corpse of another victim was found in the bazaar. 'The tiger had drunk his blood but not eaten his flesh, and they say this is what it does with men.' Ibn Battuta goes on to report dark rumours that this was perhaps all the doing of yogis, not animals at all.

Chinese Chickens

Ibn Battuta has tales of the great size of the chickens in China: 'This is nonsense' says Beckingham. Ibn Battuta had claimed that 'We bought a hen which we wanted to cook, but it would not fit into one pot: we used two'—'and as for the cocks: the first time I saw a Chinese cock was in the city of Kawlam. I thought it was an ostrich and was astonished.' As compared with the scrawny fowls of his native North Africa, no doubt any selectively bred and systematically fattened bird would have seemed huge, but it would never approach the dimensions of an ostrich! This is in all probability a traveller's tale. Certainly in that category is the sighting of the *rukhkh*.

The Roc or rukhkh

Mariners' tales of the existence of a bird of very great size were not the invention of Ibn Battuta. With the spelling *roc* it is familiar even in the West from tales such as *Sinbad the Sailor*. The Chinese crew of the junk on which he was sailing back to India became 'alarmed' when a great storm in the South China sea swept them off course into totally unfamiliar waters. They would have turned back for home, 'but that was out of the question'. Then, at dawn on the forty-third day, they spied 'a mountain projecting from the sea at a distance of 20 miles'. The sailors were puzzled, and said, 'We are nowhere near land, and there is no record of a mountain in the sea. If the wind drives us on it, we are lost.' The wind abated, and

later on when the sun rose we saw that the mountain had risen in the air, and that daylight was visible between it and the sea. We were amazed at this, and I saw the crew weeping, and taking farewell of one another. So I said, 'What is the matter with you?' They replied, 'What we thought was a mountain is the Rukh, and if it sees us it will make an end of us.' We were at that moment ten miles from it. Just then God of His mercy sent us a favourable wind, which turned us in another direction, so that we did not see it and could not learn its true shape.

Note that the effect of light described could easily have been some kind of mirage. The *interpretation* put on what was seen was not Ibn Battuta's, but the sailors'. He actually passes no judgement himself at all, and explicitly says he 'could not learn its true shape.' Almost always when one analyses one of the unusual phenomena mentioned in the *Travels*, one finds that Ibn Battuta has in one or more ways distanced himself from the story, which he quite properly is recording for us. I am not suggesting that Ibn Battuta is in some way an arch if crypto-sceptic. He was prepared to believe that a number of unusual things were possible, but, and this is what is important, he usually avoids asserting as being incontrovertibly true what is mere hearsay. His *Travels* inform us reliably that some sailors in the South China Seas in his days believed in the roc/*rukhkh*. He does not tell us that he actually sighted the giant bird.

9

Women and children

Ibn Battuta has cause to remark on the status or characteristics of women at many points on his journey. He judged what he found from the viewpoint of a man of his day, of course, and from that of an orthodox Sunni man of the law; he deplored any departure from the strictest interpretation of the Shari'a. As he travelled across the Islamic world in the first half of the fourteenth century, he did not find uniformity. Probably what amazed him most was what he saw among Berbers in his native Africa. Ibn Battuta was of Berber origin himself, although from what was in his day, as nowadays, the Arabic-speaking coastal fringe of the Moroccan Rif. It was the women of tribes that dwelt deep in the Sahara desert, at Iwalatan (in modern Mauritania) and elsewhere that surprised, and even shocked him most.

It is a commonplace of ethnographic descriptions of the Saharan Berbers, Tuareg and others, that their womenfolk, particularly the women of noble descent (and this is a people with a rigidly structured social hierarchy) enjoy great respect, and a liberty in their personal relations which is quite without parallel in the Islamic world. As Ibn Battuta remarks,

This is a thing which I have seen nowhere in the world except among the Indians of Malabar. But those are heathens; *these* people are Muslims, punctilious in observing the hours of prayer, studying books of law, and memorizing the Koran. Yet their women show no bashfulness before men, and do not veil themselves, though they are assiduous in attending the prayers.

What really scandalized our seasoned traveller was the freedom of movement and association which these women enjoyed within their community (they did not go away from home: 'they do not travel with their husbands, and even if one desired to do so, her family would not allow her to go').

The women there have 'friends' and 'companions' amongst the men outside their own families, and the men in the same way have 'companions' amongst the women of other families. A man may go into his house and find his wife entertaining her 'companion', but he takes no objection to it. One day at Iwalatan I went into the qadi's house, after asking his permission to enter, and found with him a young woman of remarkable beauty. When I saw her I was shocked, and turned to go out, but she laughed at me, instead of being overcome by shame, and the qadi said to me "Why are you going out? She is my 'companion.' 'I was amazed at their conduct, for he was a theologian, and a pilgrim to boot. I was told that he had asked the sultan's permission to make the pilgrimage that year with his 'companion' (whether this one or not I cannot say) but the sultan would not grant it.

This last item of tittle-tattle reported by Ibn Battuta is mere hearsay, but his general description of social relations between Tuareg men and women is in line with all authoritative reports, and it is not, as some of his early readers must have suspected, just another of his traveller's tales. One can understand how bewildered he must have been. With no hope of the sort of hospitality gifts which he might have expected in wealthier lands (the height of hospitality in the desert was to serve a sort of milky porridge), he beat a hasty retreat: 'I decided to make the journey to Málli, which is reached in twenty-four days from Iwálátan, if the traveller pushes on rapidly.'

We can form some idea of Ibn Battuta's standards of female beauty from the following observation on the subject of the Berber Bardama tribe:

Their women are the most perfectly beautiful of women, and they have the most elegant figures: they are pure white and very fat. I have not seen in any country any who are as fat. They feed on cows' milk and pounded millet, which they drink mixed with water, uncooked, night and morning.

The custom of fattening up nubile females in this way certainly continues into modern times; the probable harmful effects of the resulting obesity on the life expectation of women subjected to such regimes have understandably given health workers cause for concern, but that has not persuaded the girls in Mali to slim. Once again Ibn Battuta's powers of observation merit our respect.

In the Turkish lands also he finds women occupying a respected position, unveiled and with relative social freedom. He does not seem shocked by what he found there, rather full of admiration:

'A remarkable thing which I saw in this country [he was at Majar not far from Astrakhan] was the respect shown to women by the Turks, for they hold a more dignified position than the men.' He describes how a 'princess', her train carried by her attendant maidens, approached the emir 'in a stately manner'. When she reached him, 'he rose before her, and greeted her, and sat her beside him, with the maidens standing round her.' As for the merchant class, the women wear their finery in public, a conical headdress incrusted with pearls, and surmounted with peacock feathers.

The windows of the tent are open, for the Turkish women do not veil themselves. Sometimes a woman will be accompanied by her husband, and anyone would take him for one of her servants: he has no garment other than a sheep's wool cloak and a high cap to match.

Why is Ibn Battuta willing to accept among the Turks something very similar to what he finds unacceptable among the Tuareg? Could it be that the ruler of the Turks he was to visit, Sultan Muhammad Uzbek Khan was 'one of the seven mighty kings of the world', so Turks had the power to set their own standards, whereas the Berbers of the deep Sahara and the Sahel were impoverished nomads, and so should have known better?

IBN BATTUTA'S OWN WOMEN

Ibn Battuta seems rarely to have lacked for female companionship while on his travels. There is nothing to indicate that there was any whiff of adverse gossip about his conduct; as a lawyer who in more than one place was appointed as judge, qadi, we would expect him to adhere closely to the Islamic code in this as in other respects, and he did. The lawfulness of having four wives, combined with the ease of divorce, meant that as he moved about he must in series have had a large number. In his account of his travels he frequently has cause to mention his marriages or divorces, but clearly he does not seek to provide an exhaustive listing of all his spouses, so that it is quite impossible to attempt statistics.

If we can assume his practice with regard to marriages was in accordance with the Shari'a, it must be said that the suspicion does arise that he failed in his obligations with regard to maintenance of his offspring. The duty of the husband to pay maintenance (*nafaqa*) to divorced wives and such children as he has had by wives he has divorced, cannot be in doubt. There are passages in the Qur'an which deal quite specifically with such eventualities as a man divorcing a wife who is carrying his child: 'spend your substance on them [i.e. maintain them] until they are delivered, and if they suckle your child, give them recompense. And take mutual counsel together, according to what is just and reasonable' (*Surat al-Talaq*—speaking of divorced wives who are pregnant). On the same subject in *Surat al-Baqara* the requirement is: 'Mothers shall give suck to children for two whole years, if the father desires to complete the term, but he shall bear the cost of their food and clothing on equitable terms'. Maintenance is, of course, dealt with in all standard textbooks, including the *Risala* of Ibn Abi Zayd al-Qayrawani, the widely used elementary manual of Maliki law that will certainly have been familiar to Ibn Battuta. As a modern manual[1] puts it: 'As for the child, its nursing, welfare and the home of the mother remains the duty of the father.' Nowhere are we told anything of the arrangements made for the children Ibn Battuta left behind him at various stages of his journey. One might take the attitude that one ought to give him the benefit of the doubt, and assume that he had indeed taken 'mutual counsel' and set up just and reasonable arrangements, but how can he have done so if he remained totally unaware whether he had had a child by that divorced wife or not?

One case where he does mention remitting money to one of the women he left behind reflects no credit on him. On his journey out eastwards in 1326 he must have married a lady in Damascus, although in his discreet way he does not even mention the fact in his initial narrative. On his way back westwards, twenty years later, when he reaches Damascus again, as he tells us, he enquires after his son, for whom he had sent funds: 'While I was in India I learnt that she had given birth to a male child. I *had then sent forty Indian gold dinars* for his mother to his grandfather, who was from Miknasa [Meknes] in the Maghreb' (emphasis added). Was this really the best way of sending money for a child in Damascus? He was told the child had died twelve years earlier. That implies that he died at the age of about eight. Perhaps Ibn Battuta had fulfilled his duties as a father to provide for his maintenance up to that point, but it is impossible to escape from the conclusion that, if he did not know whether the child was alive or dead, he can have done nothing for him.

Are we judging, Ibn Battuta's conduct by inappropriate standards? It may well be the case that the way Ibn Battuta faced up to his parental responsibilities was no different from the way that most others in his situation did at that time. It would be wrong to single him out as notably remiss in this respect, but it would surely be equally wrong to ignore altogether such an important side of his character.

Ibn Battuta is particularly forthcoming on his marital

---

[1] A.R. Doi. *Shari'ah, the Islamic Law* (London: Ta-Ha Publishers, 1984), 206.

experiences in the Maldive Islands. Some months after leaving the islands for the first time, and being put ashore penniless on the Malabar Coast by the 'infidels with twelve warships' who had captured the vessel in which he had been sailing away from Fattan (an unidentified port on the Coromandel Coast), Ibn Battuta got to hear in Calicut about what had been going on in the Maldives. Apart from news of Maldivian politics, he heard that his wife, whom he had left pregnant, had given birth to a son.

It is easy to get married in these islands [he had told us] on account of the smallness of the dowries and the pleasure of their women's society. The majority of people do not specify a dowry. ...When ships arrive, the crews marry wives, and when they want to sail they divorce them. It is really a sort of temporary marriage, and the women never leave their country.

What needs to be borne in mind here is that 'temporary marriage', although a phenomenon not unknown in some parts of the Islamic world, is a practice very strongly condemned indeed by the orthodox Maliki school to which Ibn Battuta belonged. We have seen that he did try to modify one local custom, concerning female dress, but there is no indication that he set out to eradicate the custom of temporary marriage. Indeed he committed himself to marriages which *de facto* must have been of the temporary *mutʻa* type of which his *madhhab* (school of law) disapproved. Whatever was the external legal form of the marriages he made on the island of Muluk, if, as he says 'I stayed seventy days at Muluk, and married two wives there,' he can hardly have intended a permanent marriage.

Of the women of the Maldives he tells us that 'I have never found any women in the world more agreeable to consort with than they are.' We may take him at his word, for he tells us 'I married several women there.'

One of the ways in which our traveller classifies women is according to their aptitude for, and skill in, sexual intercourse. On his journey southwards from Delhi, for example, at a place somewhere north of Gwalior called 'Marh' (there is no point in this context in attempting to untangle an alleged itinerary which continues to puzzle investigators), his admiration for the local women leads him into a recapitulation: 'This town takes its name from the Malawa, a tribe of Hindus of powerful build, great size and fine figures; *their womenfolk* are exceedingly beautiful and famous for their charms in intercourse, and the amount of pleasure they give. So also are the women of the Marhata [Maratha] and of the Maldive Islands.'

As illuminating as his attitudes to his own wives and ex-wives was his handling, as a judge, of the marital affairs of others. He was shocked at the way that, in the Maldive Islands, divorced women had been allowed to live on in their former husband's home until they themselves remarried. This must have been a local custom of which the function was presumably to make sure that the divorced woman was not left destitute. It contravened the Shari'a, however, for the code forbids such practices, presumably in order to eliminate illicit sexual relations between the former spouses. 'The first bad custom I changed [in the Maldives] was the practice of divorced wives staying in the houses of their former husbands, for they all do so till they marry another husband.' 'I soon put that to rights. About twenty-five men who had acted thus were brought before me; I had them beaten and paraded in the bazaars, and the women put away from them'. He says nothing of making any provision for the material hardships that will have arisen for some of the women when the old order was so suddenly changed.

TABOOS ON EATING IN PUBLIC

In very many societies there are taboos which forbid one group from eating in the sight of others. More usually it is a matter of females not eating before males, but there are many permutations. There may be a ban on high-caste folk eating before inferiors, for example, but almost always there is some element of setting up boundaries between the sexes. It is interesting to watch Ibn Battuta's reactions when he encounters this taboo in his own home. Of his own wives he tells us 'some of them ate with me *after some effort on my part*, but some of them never did so, nor was I able to see them eating, and no ruse of mine for this purpose succeeded.' The frustration of a husband unable to impose his will on his women is very apparent. Ibn Battuta, the qadi anxious to impose his belief system on the islands, is unable to modify this manifestation of the local ways in his own house.

WITCHCRAFT

As noted in the chapter on religion, accusations of witchcraft were levelled more commonly against females: *kaftar*, the name he gives as the North Indian term for a witch (it is the Persian word for hyena) is only applicable to women, not men, for example.

FEMALE NUDITY

In many parts of the world on his travels Ibn Battuta came across female nudity. His attitude to this, for him, unfamiliar phenomenon, differed of course according to whether the naked women were pagans or Muslims. With Muslims he sought, where he had the power to do so, to introduce clothing. In the Maldives, the custom, when he arrived, was for women to go about with only an apron 'from the navel to the ground', but with the rest of the body uncovered. 'When I was qadi there I tried to put an end to this practice, and ordered them to wear clothes, but I met with no success.' He was, of course, able to insist that women should wear full clothing in his presence in the court of law, 'but apart from that I was unable to effect anything'.

EDUCATION FOR WOMEN

Ibn Battuta wanted to have his female slaves educated: where the local market did not provide a supply of such females, he complained. It is less clear what he felt about education for free women, but the phenomenon was in any case most unusual. Of Honavar (some distance to the south of Goa), he reports that

'The women of this town and all the coastal districts wear nothing but loose unsewn garments, one end of which they gird round their waists, and drape the rest over their head and shoulders [obviously saris]. They are beautiful and virtuous, and each wears a gold ring in her nose. One peculiarity amongst them is that they all know the Koran by heart. I saw in the town thirteen schools for girls and twenty-three for boys, a thing which I have never seen elsewhere.'

MARRIAGE AMONG THE HINDUS

The institution of suttee (he does not use the word himself) horrifies Ibn Battuta, but he is fascinated by it, and deals with it at length.

The burning of the wife after her husband's death is regarded by them as a commendable act, but is not compulsory, only when a widow burns herself her family acquire a certain prestige by it and gain a reputation for fidelity. A widow who does not burn herself dresses in coarse garments and lives with her own people in misery, despised for her lack of fidelity.

Ibn Battuta describes one such act of self-immolation which he witnessed at Amjhera. The pyre was already blazing as the widow arrived, and 'so that she should not be frightened by the sight of it', it was being 'screened off by a blanket'. The widow pulled the blanket to one side: 'I know there is a fire, so let me alone.' And 'with her hands above her head in salutation to the fire, she cast herself into it.' What Ibn Battuta does not tell us is how he came to understand what was said: he never claims to know any of the Indian vernaculars. Nevertheless he does seem to be reporting at first hand: would he have invented the detail of the woman making *puja* as she committed suicide?

10

The religious framework

The Western reader of Ibn Battuta's *Travels* would have no difficulty in getting into focus way the traveller approaches religions other than his own, but may well have problems when it comes to seeking to understand Ibn Battuta's attitude towards his own religion in its various manifestations. Non-Muslims in the West too often regard Islam as a single monolithic religious structure, and although there may be some awareness of the existence of certain lines of differentiation between one group of Muslims and another (between Sunnis and Shi'is, for example), in general there may be little understanding of any finer points of Islamic theology. But Ibn Battuta was precisely a scholar of the Islamic sciences, a professional lawyer trained in the religious code. His travels took him across the whole breadth of the Islamic world as it existed in his day. Although he did not go out of his way to seek the company of people guilty in his view of heresy, nevertheless the circumstances of travel inevitably brought him up against a very wide range of kinds of Muslim, some orthodox, some not. If we are to calibrate correctly this observer's responses to his own Islamic world, in order to decide whether we may safely rely on his observations, it is necessary to have some grasp of his own personal religious standpoint, to know the sort of Muslim that he was himself.

Perhaps it is better not to start at the chronological beginning with his education in his native North Africa in the first quarter of the fourteenth century (CE), but to pass on to his encounter in Damascus with the most outstanding of all the many religious leaders of whom he speaks: Ibn Taymiyya. Ibn Taymiyya is still a name of some potency nowadays, amongst other things because the rigorist reformation which drew much of its inspiration from his teaching, and from his voluminous writings, was later to give rise to the Wahhabi movement, and that is still a powerful force in Arabia and elsewhere.

Ibn Battuta, after a physical description of Damascus which cannot all have been based on eye-witness observations (it is largely drawn from the much earlier work of Ibn Jubayr), proceeds to give us some truly first-hand information on religious affairs in the city at the time he was there.

One of the principal Hanbalite doctors at Damascus was Taqi ad-Din ibn Taymiya, a man of great ability and wide learning, but with some kink in his brain. [Gibb's expressive translation, in 1929—it perhaps goes beyond the Arabic *'illa an fi 'aqlihi shayan* of the original.] The people of Damascus idolized him. He used to preach to them from the pulpit, and one day he made some statement that the other theologians disapproved; they carried the case to the sultan, and in consequence Ibn Taymiyya was imprisoned for some years. While he was in prison he wrote a commentary on the Koran, which he called *The Ocean*, in about forty volumes. Later on his mother presented herself before the sultan and interceded for him, so he was set at liberty, until he did the same thing again. I was in Damascus at the time and attended the service which he was conducting one Friday, as he was addressing and admonishing the people from the pulpit. In the very midst of his discourse he said 'Verily God descends to the sky over our world [from Heaven] in the same bodily fashion that I make this descent, and stepped down one step of the pulpit. A Malikite doctor present contradicted him and objected to his statement, but the common people rose up against this doctor, and beat him with their hands and shoes so severely that his turban fell off, and disclosed a silken skull-cap on his head. Inveighing against him for wearing this, they haled him before the qadi of the Hanbalites, who ordered him to be imprisoned, and afterwards had him beaten. The other doctors objected to this treatment and carried the matter before the principal amir, who wrote to the sultan about the matter and at the same time drew up a legal attestation against Ibn Taymiyya for various heretical pronouncements. This deed was sent on to the sultan, who gave orders that Ibn Taymiyya should be imprisoned in the citadel, and there he remained until his death.

That is a tendentious, partially misleading, and incomplete account of the situation, but it takes us into the heart of a number of the conflicts raging at this time, conflicts that helped define the spiritual and intellectual world in which Ibn Battuta moved. They were not conflicts in which Ibn Battuta chose to involve himself if he could avoid doing so, whereas Ibn Taymiyya, as may be inferred even from the brief extract above, was not the sort of person who would avoid head-on conflict where he felt that a question of religious principle was at stake.

Ibn Taymiyya (b. 1263) is described as a Hanbali. This refers to his adherence to the juridical school (*madhhab*) of Ibn Hanbal (b. 780). Ibn Battuta's *madhhab*, equally orthodox, was that of Malik ibn Anas: the Maliki *madhhab*. In Sunni Islam there are four such schools, all of undisputed orthodoxy, and in some contexts they have been and still are able to concert their statements, but that does not mean that there are no differences between them at all sorts of levels. In his preaching, Ibn Taymiyya called for refutation of the rationalist explanation of the Qu'ran and traditions, and for an end to the sort of ingenious logic-chopping which sought to explain away, for example, phrases in the holy text apparently tending to anthropomorphism (the ascription to God of attributes of a limited human nature: *tashbih*). In general he called for a rejection of all theological innovation in a drive to return to the righteousness of Islam's beginnings. He was for this reason loud in his condemnation of the cult of holy men (*awliya'*), and of the making of pilgrimages to their tombs. If the first of these themes present in his preaching, puritanical fundamentalism, brought him into conflict with many Islamic theologians (the broad class of scholars—*'ulama'*—to which Ibn Battuta himself belonged), the second brought conflict with mystics (Sufis), for among the more important reasons for the growing hold Sufism had over the religion of the people were cults centred on places where holy men were buried. Ibn Taymiyya's denunciation of such innovations, which he styled idolatrous, made him many enemies, as did the inflexible and uncompromising stance which he adopted in his polemics. The accusation of anthropomorphism was brought against him early, and no doubt arose from his reluctance ever to depart from, or detract from, the plain, literal sense of God's revealed word (in which there does appear apparently anthropomorphic language such as that to which Ibn Battuta refers in the passage quoted). He would not explain away expressions (such as 'the hand of God') which might pose difficulties, but insisted on retaining them in their integrity. If the words were in the holy text, that should be sufficient. So when, in the sermon at which Ibn Battuta claims to have been present, Ibn Taymiyya, repeated his uncompromising statement of beliefs, he had already served prison sentences for this and other offences of 'heresy'. In prison once again in 1326, as a result of the occasion to which Ibn Battuta refers, Ibn Taymiyya at first was able to continue his writing, but when the authorities realized what he was doing, they deprived him of even the resource of pen and paper; before the month was out, he was dead.

Such was the respect he inspired in Damascus that it is said his funeral was attended by 200,000 men and 15,000 women. Ibn Battuta does not mention any of this, he concentrates on the incident of the Maliki scholar (Ibn al-Zahra' by name) who made so bold as to argue against him.

It is interesting to see that according to Ibn Battuta, the matter was resolved when other doctors of the law took the case before 'the principal amir'. The Arabic text actually styles him *malik al-umara*', and gives his name, Sayf al-Din Tankiz. This functionary passed the dossier on the case up to the Sultan al-Nasir. It might seem that what was at issue was the purely theological question of the attributes of God, and so that this would be a matter for the religious Shari'a court. That the incident was dealt with in the first instance by the 'principal emir' would indicate that this was deemed a public order offence, and a matter for the emir's police, rather than an issue to be brought before the qadi's court.

The *de facto* coexistence in medieval Muslim societies of the two jurisdictions, that of the qadis and that of the emirs, entailed a relationship not easy to grasp (just as it is difficult to grasp how in Christian Europe in certain periods the ecclesiastical jurisdictions, and in particular the Inquisition, meshed in with the civil power while at the same time claiming to be quite independent). There is a tension latent in this state of affairs, one which not infrequently leads a qadi to take up a position in defiance of government. Ibn Battuta was not the type of religious lawyer to go out of his way to defy state authority, but even he on occasion is to be found making a legal decision which he knew would create political problems, and sticking to that decision because it was what the Shari'a laid down. Ibn Battuta was no 'fundamentalist', but he was no relaxed liberal reformer either: he came into conflict with the non-Shari'a authorities during his periods of office in both Delhi and in the Maldives. In this latter case the secular authorities tried to steer him away from what they perceived as a harsh penalty out of line with the established custom and practice of those geographical parts, but Ibn Battuta insisted on his original sentence.

Contemporary aspirations among the pious to universalize the use of the religious code (Shari'a) in modern Islamic states lead too easily to the assumption that medieval Islamic regimes had no place for non-Shari'a jurisdictions. That was far from being the case. The division of functions is clearly signalled in many passages of the *Travels*. In Delhi Ibn Battuta tells us of a situation which arose from the distribution of food relief to the poor during a famine. This is not a normal function of a qadi, of course, but the vizier had entrusted the task to Ibn Battuta as an emergency measure during the crisis, and he seems to have carried out what he had to do with diligence. However, there existed in this society a type of belief in witchcraft according to which the consequence of a witch using his or her powers of evil eye would be the death of the victim, and if this victim were then cut open in a post mortem examination, it would be found that the corpse had no heart. It would have been eaten by the witch. A woman accused of being a witch of this type, and the dead body of a boy, her alleged victim, were brought to him one day.

How did he deal with this grave challenge? By handing them over to the jurisdiction of the emir.

I ordered them to take her to the Sultan's lieutenant who commanded that she should be put to the test. They filled four jars with water, and tied them to her hands and feet, and threw her into the river Jun [Jumna]. As she did not sink she was known to be a [witch]; had she not floated she would not have been one.

He ordered her then to he burned with fire. It is at the orders of the government official, not of the qadi, that the witch is put to death.

On the ready acceptance by Ibn Battuta of the catch-22 punishment for witches (even though it was not his direct responsibility or invention), one has to bear in mind that similar inescapable logical traps have been set at times for witches in many other cultures (including Europe and New England during the seventeenth-century witch-craze). Nevertheless, although the belief in witches was so deeply embedded in the society in which he was living and working that to stand out against it would have had little hope of success, he still had a duty to make some attempt to stop a grave punishment quite outside the Shari'a code. In the case of survivals of local customs such as infringements of the rules of modesty in dress, or of the treatment of divorced women, we have seen he was willing to make his stand. In this case not.

Mention has already been made, in connection with Ibn Taymiyya, of the tension which existed between Sufi religious practices and those of orthodox religion, particularly those of the scholars. This is no place to seek to summarize a profound debate which has gone on for so long, and which continues in various forms today. A simplistic view would be that the Islam of the Sufi mystics called in question the law as taught by the scholars, because Sufism laid stress on the primary importance of the direct access of the individual soul to the divinity, and on the primacy of religious experience (rather than on religion as ritual), on the manifestations of divine grace (*karamat*), even on miracles. Many would counter that this is an over-simplification, and would wish to point out that the way of the mystics in no way sought to invalidate the disciplines of the law, or to deny them.

Ibn Battuta signals his dual loyalty to both aspects of religion, and his refusal to become engaged in denigration of either, in what are the key passages relating to the motives which initially impelled him to take to the road, and then made him persist in what he was doing. We hear of both (and this can hardly be a matter of coincidence) during his visit in 1326 to Alexandria, his first point of contact with the Middle East. All along through North Africa he was a pious young pilgrim, but no more; from the time of this illumination (that is not too strong a term) in Alexandria, his journeys become, potentially at least, the fulfilment of a vision.

What happens to him in Alexandria provides a framework relating his subsequent travels firstly to the broad world of orthodox scholars, and then, further, within to the spiritual universe of the mystics.

First the orthodox Sunni inspiration:

One of the learned men of Alexandria was the qadi, a master of eloquence, who used to wear a turban of extraordinary size. Never, either in the eastern or the western lands have I seen a more voluminous headgear. Another of them was the pious ascetic Burhan al-Din ('the lame', *al-a'raj*), one of the greatest of ascetics, and an outstandingly devout person, whom I met in my stay, and whose hospitality I enjoyed for three days. One day, as I entered his room, he said to me, 'I see that you are fond of travelling through foreign lands.' I replied, 'Yes I am' (though I had as yet no thought of going to such distant lands as India or China). Then he said 'You must certainly visit my brother Farid al-Din in India, and my brother Rukn al-Din in Sind, and when you find them give them a greeting from me.' I was amazed at his prediction, *and the idea of going to these countries having been cast into my mind, my journeys never ceased until I met these three that he named, and conveyed his greeting to them.* [emphasis added]

Here then, at least as Ibn Battuta saw it, was how the outline of the great enterprise of his world-wide travels was formed. Then from Alexandria he sets out to visit his second mentor, the Shaykh al-Murshidi, at his rural hermitage (*zawiya*) near to Fua. We here move into a world of unambiguous mysticism. Ibn Battuta worships in company with al-Murshidi's disciples. At the end of the day he is sent up to sleep on the flat roof, on a straw mattress, covered with a leather mat. And that night in his sleep he has a vision or dream. There is no obfuscation: what he experiences is not presented as a real happening: 'it was as if (*ka-anni*)', we are told, 'I was on the wing of a great bird which was flying with me towards Makka, then to Yemen, then eastwards, and thereafter going towards the south, then flying far eastwards, and finally landing in a dark and green country, where it left me.'

Ibn Battuta asks al-Murshidi to interpret his dream:

'You will make the pilgrimage [to Makka], and visit [the tomb of] the Prophet, and you will travel through the Yemen, Iraq, the country of the Turks, and India. You will stay there a long time and meet my brother Dilshad the Indian, who will rescue you from a danger into which you will fall.'

Once again the line of Ibn Battuta's travels is projected onwards by a holy man. The device of the prophecies and the dream serve to provide a forward narrative impulse, advancing in stages, not in one single leap, from Morocco to Egypt and on further eastwards. Ibn Battuta is initially fulfilling the religious obligation of the *hajj*. From Egypt to India he proceeds, as it were further under the aegis of al-Murshidi. In India the prophecy is fulfilled, Dilshad encountered, and that mysterious figure provides the traveller with the Quranic formula: 'Say, God is sufficient for us, and an excellent guardian.' He repeats this over and over, one might almost say, as we are in India, like a mantra, and survives to complete his programme of journeying. The third stage of this relay of mystic support came in Assam, where, in the Kamaru mountains, as we have seen, he went to visit Shaykh Jalal al-Din, and the fourth in China in Beijing, where Ibn Battuta sought out the hospice where Burhan al-Din resided. There the traveller found that miraculously the fine goat hair garment originally entrusted to him had been safely delivered. And it was this same Burhan al-Din who advised Ibn Battuta to leave China and begin his journey home, thus closing the circle. At times Ibn Battuta's fascination with material gain is overwhelming, embarrassing to his readers, but the underlying structure and the direction (in all senses of the word) of his travels was nevertheless religious, and he leaves us in no doubt about that.

It may be objected that if we take this view of the *Travels*, then what comes after the prophecies are accomplished becomes extraneous. From Morocco to Morocco has brought the traveller full circle already under the aegis of his Sufi master. Nothing after that (Spain, the Sahara, the lands of the bend of the Niger) was 'predicted', and so the traveller departs from the pattern originally set, goes far beyond it. Pure wanderlust seems to take over.

Travelling did not get any easier in the Maghreb as he approached his final goal, Fez. Indeed, as he is driven to tell us, for the last stage of all:

I set out on December 29 at a time of intense cold, and snow fell very heavily all the way. I have in my life seen bad roads, and quantities of snow, at Bukhara and Samarkand, in Khorasan and the lands of the Turks, but never have I seen anything worse than the road of Umm Junayba.

That was a mere 90 kilometres from home and provides the narrative with a final moment of suspense. However, there in Fez, 'I settled down under the wing of his [Abu 'Inan's] bounty after long journeying.'

It is without any great confidence that the reader formulates the hope that the traveller did indeed enjoy the 'ample favours and ample benefits which he has bestowed on me'.

The malady of wanderlust is usually incurable.

Postscript

Unless otherwise indicated, translations in this study are based on those of Sir Hamilton Gibb as completed by Professor Charles Beckingham, but it should perhaps first be said that, although he was my teacher, Gibb did not lecture on Ibn Battuta, so I did not have the benefit of his formal instruction on this subject, nor did I, to the best of my recollection, ever have the opportunity of discussing Ibn Battuta with him, even though he was the supervisor of my postgraduate studies. I can in no way claim, therefore, that the views I express here are, even in an indirect way, a reflection of any unpublished opinions of his. My immense debt to him is, where Ibn Battuta is concerned, exclusively to his published works. The interpretation is mine alone.

We are fortunate to have now available the complete text of the five-volume Hakluyt Society English translation of *The Travels of Ibn Battuta*. Gibb brought out volume I as long ago as 1958, but as Professor Charles Beckingham makes clear in his Foreword to volume IV (1994), the history of this project goes back very much further than that. The original proposal for the translation of the whole of the *Travels* was actually made in 1922, and Gibb's one-volume selection of texts appeared in the Broadway Travellers series in 1929 (second edition, 1954). Gibb died in 1971, before he had completed the task. Volume II had come out in 1962. By 1971 Gibb was extremely ill, and volume III was seen through its final stages with the assistance of Professor Charles Beckingham, who was eventually persuaded to take over and finish what had been started so long before, but was not for some considerable time free to begin active work on the completion of volume IV, which only appeared in 1994. The final volume of notes and bibliography at last appeared in 2000. (As he wryly remarked, the translation had already by that time taken twice as long as the travels themselves.) Sadly Beckingham died in 1998, and the project could only be completed thanks to Professor A. D. H. Bivar who, in 2000, stepped in and provided Volume V, an index. (The original plan envisaging further studies had to be abandoned.)

Now we at last have the Hakluyt Society translation, why not use it? I certainly have done that, but it seems to me that one needs to take account of the consequences that flow from the abnormally long period of gestation. The Broadway Travellers text of 1929 was produced when the project was still fresh, and when Gibb was still a young man. It is reasonable to suppose that some passages must have actually been translated already, even well before he made his initial proposal to the Hakluyt Society in 1922. Work on the later parts of the book continued when, as Beckingham points out, Gibb was already a sick man, and exhausted. Volume III Beckingham sees as 'evidence of great courage and determination, as well as impressive scholarship'. It is not surprising that in its style the Broadway Travellers version should in places seem, to me at least, tauter, livelier, and since the extracts chosen by Gibb range across the whole work, it is not surprising that coherence of tone is achieved without difficulty. I do not know whether I am alone in regretting that, sometimes, the felicitous vigour of 1929 should fade a little in the more complete and more painstaking final version. For this reason I am unwilling to set the earlier text on one side altogether, although one certainly cannot envisage ignoring the product of the mature reflections of Gibb and Beckingham.

There is also the problem of place names and proper names. It is not only that in 1929 Routledge and Kegan Paul employed simplified transliterations, with no subscript dots, and a grave accent to indicate vowel length, whereas the Hakluyt Society provide the full panoply of Arabist diacritics. There is also the question of 'familiar' names. That Gibb should have preferred to write Alexandria is understandable; after all, he knew how to write in English the name of the city where he was born. On other names it has to be said that his practice with such names varied. In 1929 he had written Delhi, but Beckingharn makes it clear that it was Gibb's own expressed wish that in 1971 and 1994 the form was Dihli. In contradiction with this approach, in 1929 we find Gharnata (explained as Granada, but with the 'Arabic' form the predominant one in main text), whereas in 1994 we have Granada (in one of the sections which it must have fallen to Beckingham to complete). Such variation would prove confusing in a short work such as this. Where one of the 1929 extracts is used, place names are brought into line with what is found in the 1958–94 volumes, but (and this is an important exception), if a thoroughly familiar English form is available, it is adopted. For all these and other reasons the translations are 'based on' but do not necessarily always follow Gibb and Beckingham. For publication in such a short and sparsely annotated volume as this, the prime consideration has been to choose a version capable of communicating the sense immediately and unambiguously. For the translations, therefore, I must take all the responsibility where they are imperfect, but none of the credit where they succeed.

Further reading

This section does not set out to provide a complete survey of writings on Ibn Battuta. The volume is an introductory one, and its principal aim must be to send readers to the text, to convince them that the *Travels* is a work that deserves to be read complete. The following remarks are, therefore, restricted to information on the basic text itself, together with some indication of the rich variety of studies which have appeared in recent years, in the hope that these will provide an initial opening to Ibn Battuta studies for those who wish to journey further with the great traveller.

TEXT

The scholarly edition on which most modern studies of Ibn Battuta rely is: C. Defrémy and B.R. Sanguinetti (eds), *Voyages d'Ibn Batoutah*, Paris, 1874–9, 4 vols., 3rd edn., 1893–5. It provides the Arabic text as well as a French translation (the French translation was reprinted with notes etc., by Vincent Monteil, Paris: Editions Anthropos, 1968). It was on this Defrémy and Sanguinetti edition of the Arabic that Gibb and Beckingharn based their translations (see below). Editions which have appeared in the modern Arab world likewise usually stem from Defrémy and Sanguinetti. For this volume I have used: *Rihla Ibn Battuta. 1305/*

1985. (Beirut: Dar Bayrut li-l-Tiba'a wa-l-Nashr), 1960. It has a short introduction by Karam al-Bustani, 5–7.

In English we have:

Ibn Battuta, *Travels in Asia and Africa, 1325–1354*. Translated and selected by H.A.R. Gibb, (London: Routledge and Kegan Paul, Broadway Travellers), 1929.

The Travels of Ibn Battuta AD *1325–1354*. Translated with revisions and notes from the Arabic text edited by C. Defrémy and B.R. Sanguinetti by H.A.R. Gibb (London: The Hakluyt Society), vol. i, 1958; ii, 1962; iii, 1971; iv, the translation completed with annotations by C.F. Beckingham, 1994. Volume V, Index, compiled by A.D.W. Bivar, 2000.

Tim Mackintosh-Smith describes his edition of *The Travels of Ibn Battutah* (Picador, 2002) as 'abridged, introduced and annotated' by himself. The basic text he employs is that of Gibb and Beckingham (see above), and to this he adheres very closely. The abridgement is achieved by judicious excision of whole passages that serve purposes other than that of carrying the main travel narrative forward. At Makka, for example, some 16 pages of the section describing the holy sites and ceremonies are omitted, as are most of the discussion of individual scholars and notables there. (In general this abridgement gives more detail than Gibb did in his 1929 version: there are 296 pages of text and twenty-three of notes). *The Travels of Ibn Battutah* (2002) will probably now be the most easily accessible and convenient version for English-speaking readers.

RECENT STUDIES

Associated with Mackintosh-Smith's abridgement of Gibb and Beckingham are his two travel books: *Travels with a Tangerine* (John Murray, 2001 and in paperback Picador, 2002) and *The Hall of a Thousand Columns* (John Murray, 2005). The first of these has as its subtitle *A Journey in the Footnotes of Ibn Battutah*. This might convey the impression that the book is exclusively concerned with the elucidation of textual problems. There certainly is a good deal of high-level discussion of points of detail, but there is also an engaging (sometimes a trifle jokey) treatment of his own travels (which, as much as Mackintosh-Smith's scholarship, probably accounts for the book's success). The first of these two travel books follows in Ibn Battuta's footsteps from North Africa to the Middle East, and the second deals almost exclusively with the Indian Subcontinent as far as the Malabar coast. Whether further volumes are to be expected on China and on Africa is not made clear.

R.E. Dunn, *The Adventures of Ibn Battuta: A Muslim Traveller of the Fourteenth Century* (London and Sydney: Croom Helm), 1986. See also the same author's 'International Migrations of Literate Muslims in the Later Middle Ages: the Case of Ibn Battuta', in Netton (ed.),1993, 75–85 (see below).

S. Hamdun and N. King, *Ibn Battuta in Black Africa* (Princeton, NJ: Markus Wiener Publishers), 1994. A reprint with a new Foreword by Ross E. Dunn, of a study which first appeared in 1975.

The following volumes are not exclusively on Ibn Battuta, but contain a number of important recent studies on him, and provide valuable references to further recent publications in this area:

D.F. Eickelman and J. Piscatori, *Muslim Travellers: Pilgrimage, Migration and the Religious Imagination* (Berkeley/Los Angeles: University of California Press), 1990.

I.R. Netton, *Golden Roads, Migration, Pilgrimage and Travel in Mediaeval and Modern Islam* (Richmond, Surrey: Curzon Press), 1993.

Finally, I wish to mention a little work on Ibn Battuta with an approach very different from my own. In *The Travels of Ibn Battuta* (Cambridge: Hood Hood Books), Abdel al-Rahman Azzam is writing in the first place 'for children between the ages of 6–9', but, thanks in part to the quality of the illustrations (by Khaled Sayeb) and to the clarity of his own style, he succeeds in conveying the hold that this narrative still has over imaginations.

Index

'Abbadan, 19
'Abdallah ibn Khafif, 90–1
'Abdallah, vizier, 38–9
Abu 'Abdallah b. 'Asim, 54
Abu 'Abdallah b. Ghalib, 56
Abu 'Inan, 5, 52
Abu l-Barakat al-Barbari, 33
Abu l-Hasan 'Ali al-Anjuri, 18
Abu l-Hasan, the Marinid, 63
Abu l-Muzaffar Hasan, 67
Abu l-Qasim Muhammad, 54
Abu Sa'id Bahadur Khan, 82
Acre, 20
Adam's Peak (Ceylon), 90
Afghanistan, 24–5
Afghans, 25
Africans: *see* black(s).
agriculture, 36
Ahmad al-Mansur, Muley, 69
Alexandria, 80, 113–14, 118
Alfonso XI of Castile, 53
Algeciras, 51, 62–3
Alhambra, 58, 66
'Ali ibn Abi Talib, 51
'aja'ib, 5, 62, 90

Aligarh: *see* Kuwil
'alim, 66, 87
ambition, 24, 33, 68
Amjhera, 106
al-Andalus, 53–4, 56, 58, 60–2, 65
Andronicus III, Emperor, 23
animals, 90–7
Arabian peninsula, 15, 66, 68
Asilah, 66
Assam, 114
Astrakhan, 24–5, 100
Atabeg, 81
Aydhab, 15, 20
Azerbayjan, 66
Azov, Sea of, 72

Baghdad, 18, 51, 80, 82
Bardama (Berber tribe): *see* Berber tribes
bards, tribal, 57, 72
Basra, 19, 51, 81
Beckingham, Charles, 9, 22–3, 42, 57, 74, 95, 116–20
Bengal, 85–6
Berber tribes, 52, 64, 70, 98–9, 101

INDEX

Bethlehem, 23
Bijaya, 14
black(s), 14, 35, 38, 46, 66, 68–9, 74, 94–5
Black Death, the, 52
Black Sea, the, 42
Black Stone, the, 16
'bombards', 63
bride-price, 80
'Bridle, the' (Sufi hospice), 65
Bukhara, 115
Bulghar, 21, 48
Burhan al-Din, 113–15

Cairo, 20, 52
Calicut, 103
cannibalism, 73–4
carrion, eating of, 73–4
Castilian Christian forces, 61, 63
celebrity, cult of, 4, 9
Ceuta, 53, 62, 66
Ceylon (Sri Lanka), 33, 86, 90, 93–4
chickens, 95
children, 39–40, 52, 91, 98, 101–3
China, vii, 8, 30, 48–52, 57, 59, 84, 87, 89, 95–7, 113–15, 121; embassy to, 8, 30, 41–7
coconut, 33, 36, 86
coir, 36
Constantine (Algeria), 80
Constantinople, 22–4, 59, 72
cowrie shells, 85–6
crocodiles, 94–5
Cyprus, 21

Damascus, 7, 15–16, 51–2, 56–7, 80, 102, 108, 110
Damietta, 80

Dawlatabad, 27–8, 31
Delhi, 25–8, 31, 34–5, 42, 44–7, 59, 66, 69, 71, 83–4, 88, 103, 111, 118
Dilshad, 19, 46, 114
diplomacy, diplomat(ic), 41, 43, 47, 88–9
divorce, 37–8, 101–4, 112
Dome of the Rock, 23
Don Quixote, 43–4
dowry, 37, 103
dust, scattering over the head, 72

'Eagle, the' (Sufi hospice), 65
Edhfu, 20
education for women, 105–6
Egypt, 8–9, 15, 19, 21, 46, 67, 81, 93, 114
elephant, 90–92

Farbá Husayn, 70
Farid al-Din, 113
Fattan, 103
Fez, 5, 52, 54, 64, 66, 79, 115
finance, vii, 14, 26, 79–89
fortune, 15, 24, 45, 80, 83–4, 89
Frankish Christians, 72
Fua, 19, 114
funeral rites, 50–51, 106; of Ibn Taymiyya, 110

Gawgaw (Gao), 92
George, former king, 23
Ghazna, 83
Ghiyath al-Din (of Damaghan), 38–9
Gibraltar, 10, 55–6, 59, 61–3, 66
Goa, 105

gold, 50–1, 58, 73, 80, 85–6, 102; gold dust, 69
Golden Horde, 21–2
goliards, 88
Granada, vii, 7, 53–66, 118
Greek (language), 23
griots: see bards, tribal
'Gulistan', slave-girl, 34
Gwalior, 45, 95, 103

hajj (pilgrimage), 13–16, 18–20, 24, 30, 52, 68, 71, 79–80, 82, 87, 99, 113–14, 121
al-Hajj 'Ali, 86
halal, rules of, 48, 74
Hamdun, Said, 74
Hanbali (school, rite), 108–9
hippopotamus, 92–4
holy men, cult of, 14, 18, 46, 64, 90, 109
Honavar, 105
Hormuz, 51
hospitality, 8, 19, 34, 59, 71, 73, 79, 82, 84, 99, 113
hyenas, 93

Ibadis, 71
Iberian Peninsula, 51, 53, 59
Ibn al-'Arabi, 64
Ibn al-Khatib, Lisan al-Din, 58
Ibn al-Zahra', 110
Ibn Jubayr, 7–8, 16, 56, 62, 108
Ibn Juzayy, 3, 5, 7–8, 50, 53–8, 62–3, 66
Ibn Taymiyya, 16, 108–10, 112
ihram, 80
Ilkhan, the, 82
India, 19–20, 24–33, 36, 38, 42, 44, 46–7, 51–2, 66–7, 71–2, 79, 83, 85, 91, 96, 98, 102, 113–14, 121; elephant, 92; map, 29; vernaculars, 106; witchcraft, 105
information network of scholars, 9, 18–20
Iran, 25, 66, 90
Iraq, 18–19, 52, 80–3, 114
Isfahan, 51, 82
Islamic lawyer: see lawyer
Islamic Spain: see al-Andalus
Iwalatan (Walata, Oualata), 70–1, 98–9

Jalal al-Din, Shaykh, 114
Jalal al-Din, Sultan of the Maldives, 35
jali: see bards, tribal
Jedda, 20, 52
Jerba, 52
Jerusalem, 20, 23, 52,
'Joyous Heart', 46
al-Judhami, Abu Ja'far Ahmad, 55

Ka'ba, 13, 16
Kabul, 25
kaftar (witch), 105
Kafur (the eunuch), 44–5
Kawlam, 51, 95
Khan-Baliq (Beijing), 50
Khorasan, 66, 115
Khwaja Jahan, 91
Kilwa, vii, 67
King, Noel, 74
Konya, 66
Kufa, 51
Kuwil (Aligarh), 45–7

Ladhaqiya, 20
'Land of Darkness', 21–2

INDEX 125

lawyer, 10, 18, 33, 61, 68, 82, 88–9, 101, 107, 111
leeches, 94
Leo Africanus, 33
leopard, 95
Luristan, 25, 81–2, 84
Luxor, 15, 93

Ma'bar (Coromandel Coast), 38
Macaca silenus, 93
Madina, 13, 18
Maghreb, the, 18, 33, 52, 102, 115
Mahal (Malé), 34, 36
al-Mahruq, Abu 'Abdallah Muhammad b., 65
maintenance, payment of (*nafaqa*), 101–2
Majar, 100
Makka, 13–16, 18–20, 24, 30, 52, 68, 80–1, 114, 120
Mal al-Amir, 81
Malawa (Hindu tribe), 104
Maldives, 32–40, 60, 85–6, 103–5, 111
Malik ibn Anas, 51, 109
Maliki (school, rite), 33, 37, 43, 64, 80, 84, 88, 101, 103, 108–10
Mansa Sulayman, 72–3
Manshú Jú, 71
al-Maqqari, 56
Marbella, 61–2
Marco Polo, 4, 41–2
Marh, 103
Marrakesh, 66
marriage, 25, 36, 79; 'temporary marriage' (*mut'a*), 37 103; among Hindus, 106

marriages of Ibn Battuta, 79, 101–2
Mas'ud Khan, 26
matrilineal organization, 35, 37
Melilla, 52
memorizing the Qur'an, 6, 72–3, 99
memory, cultivation of, 6–7
Miknasa (Meknes), 102
Miliana, 13–14
Mogadishu, 67
Mongols, 50
monkeys, 93–4
mosquitoes, 92, 94
Mostaganem, 52
Moussa-Mahmoud, Fatma, 8–9
Muhammad ibn Tughluq, 25, 27, 30–2, 41, 44, 83, 91
Muhammad of Herat, 44
Muhammad Uzbek Khan, *see* Özbeg
Muhammad Uzbek Khan, Sultan, 100
Muluk, 103
al-Murshidi, 19, 46, 80, 114
mut'a, *see* marriage, temporary
Muzaffariya college, 18

Najaf, 51
nakedness of women in public, 35, 43, 105
al-Nasir, Sultan, 110
Nasrid dynasty, 64–5
natural history, vii, 90
Niger (the river), vii, 67, 70, 85, 92, 94, 115
Nile, vii, 20
nubile females, fattening up of, 100
nudity, *see* nakedness
Nur al-Din Sakhawi, 80

INDEX

Özbeg, 21–3

Panj Ab (river in Sind), 93
paper money in China, 50; paper credit, 84
Persia, 24
Persian, 20, 28, 34, 46, 48, 57, 66, 105
Persian Gulf, 51
pilgrimage, 44, 90, 109; *see hajj*
porcelain, Chinese, 49
portraiture, Chinese, 49

Qan, the, 51, 59
Qarajil (the Himalayas), 44
Qayrawani, Ibn Abi Zayd al-, 101
qulb al-mas (tunny-like fish), 36
Qurtay, amir, 57, 59
Qusayr, 20

Ramadan, 21, 73
rhinoceros, 93
Rif, 98
roc (*rukhkh*), 96–7
Rukn al-Din, 113
Russians, 22, 72

Sa'adi, 57
sab' (leopard), 95
Sabika, Mount, 65
Sahara, the, 66–70, 92, 98, 101, 115
Sahel, the, 101
Salé, 66
Samarkand, 115
Sardinia, 52
Sawahil, 67
Sayf al-Din Tankiz, 110
Sfax, 79

Shari'a, 34, 39, 98, 101–2, 104, 110–12
Shihab al-Din, Shaykh, 30
Shushtar (Tustar), 81
Siberian Arctic, 22
Sijilmassa, 70
Sind, 25, 28, 83, 93, 113
sled dogs, 48; sleds drawn by dogs, 21
Sri Lanka: *see* Ceylon
Sufi, 46, 64–6, 109, 112, 115
Sumatra, 51
Sunni, 27, 37, 64, 71, 98, 107, 109, 113
suttee, 106
Swahili (language), 67
Syria, 8, 15–16, 20–1, 52, 80 (*see also:* Damascus)

taboos, 87, on eating, 104
Tajpur, 46
Tangier, vii, 13, 18, 53
Tanzania, vii, 67, 69
Tarifa, 514
'temporary marriage': *see* marriage
Tenes, 52
tigers, 95
Timbuktu, vii, 92
Tlemcen, 13, 18
tomb of the Prophet, 13, 19, 114
Tuareg, 98–100
turban, 108, 113
Turkic languages, 48
Turkish, 20, 100
Turks, 19, 100, 114–15
Tustar *see* Shushtar

Ukak, 72

Ukraine, vii, 72
'*ulama*', 109
Umm Junayba, 115

Volga, 21–2

Wahhabi movement, 108
witchcraft, 105, 111
women, vii, 33, 35–8, 74, 88, 98–106, 110, 112

Ya-Sin (sura of the Qur'an), 75

Yemen, 19–20, 36, 114
yogi, 39, 42, 44, 95
Yusuf I, 58–60

Zafar (Dhofar), 68
Zaghari, 71
Zagros mountains, 81
Zahir al-Din (of Zanjan), 44
al-Zaytun (Quanzhou), 51
Zihar (Dhar), 91
zulu (name for leeches), 94